AUSTRALIA'S CASH ECONOMY

To Bridget

Australia's Cash Economy
A troubling issue for policymakers

CHRISTOPHER BAJADA
University of Technology, Sydney

LONDON AND NEW YORK

First published 2002 by Ashgate Publishing

Reissued 2018 by Routledge
2 Park Square, Milton Park, Abingdon, Oxon OX14 4RN
711 Third Avenue, New York, NY 10017, USA

Routledge is an imprint of the Taylor & Francis Group, an informa business

Copyright © Christopher Bajada 2002

All rights reserved. No part of this book may be reprinted or reproduced or utilised in any form or by any electronic, mechanical, or other means, now known or hereafter invented, including photocopying and recording, or in any information storage or retrieval system, without permission in writing from the publishers.

Notice:
Product or corporate names may be trademarks or registered trademarks, and are used only for identification and explanation without intent to infringe.

Publisher's Note
The publisher has gone to great lengths to ensure the quality of this reprint but points out that some imperfections in the original copies may be apparent.

Disclaimer
The publisher has made every effort to trace copyright holders and welcomes correspondence from those they have been unable to contact.

A Library of Congress record exists under LC control number: 2001098004

ISBN 13: 978-1-138-73418-0 (hbk)
ISBN 13: 978-1-138-73412-8 (pbk)
ISBN 13: 978-1-315-18737-2 (ebk)

Contents

List of Figures	*vii*
List of Tables	*viii*
Preface	*x*
Acknowledgements	*xi*
List of Abbreviations	*xii*

1	Introduction	1
2	What is the Underground Economy?	17
3	Methodologies for Estimating the Underground Economy	29
4	Motivations and Consequences	41
5	Estimating the Size of the Underground Economy for Australia	57
	Appendix 5A	81
	Appendix 5B	90
	Appendix 5C	102
	Appendix 5D	104
6	Business and Household Participation	106
	Appendix 6A	133
	Appendix 6B	136

7	Measures to Combat Clandestine Activities	138
8	Concluding Remarks	166

Bibliography *172*
Index *183*

List of Figures

1.1	Discrepancies in the Estimates of the Underground Economy Abroad (1976-80)	7
1.2	Measures of Currency – Nominal and Real (1989-90) Per Capita	13
2.1	A Modified Taxonomy of Economic Activities	25
5.1	The Cash Economy in Australia (% of GDP)	70
5.2	Real Growth Rates in the Legitimate and Underground Sectors (%) 1968-96	75
5A.1	Empirical Frequency Distribution of Bootstrapped Estimates of the Underground Economy (% of GDP)	87
5A.2	Upper and Lower Bound Estimates of the Underground Economy (% of GDP)	88
6.1	Contributions by Business and Consumers to the Size of the Cash Economy in Australia (% of GDP)	117
6.2	The Federal Budget Deficit: Reducing the Tax Gap	121

List of Tables

2.1	Defining the Underground Economy	24
3.1	Underground Economy – Methodology and Estimates	37
4.1	Tax Morality Index (Germany)	49
5.1	Dickey-Fuller Unit Root Tests	61
5.2	Endogeniety Tests	63
5.3	MacKinnon-White-Davidson J-Test	64
5.4	MacKinnon-White-Davidson J-Test	64
5.5	Estimation Results	65
5.6	Properties of Residuals	66
5.7	Measure of Robustness – Excess Sensitivity in Taxes and Welfare Benefits	67
5.8	Comparative Estimates of the Underground Economy (% of GDP)	74
5.9	Correlation and Covariance	77
5.10	Granger Causality Tests	77
5.11	Growth Rates of Real Income in Each Sector: Means and Variances	78
5A.1	Interval Estimates of the Underground Economy	86
5B.1	Legitimate Classical Business Cycle Dates for Australia: Real Seasonally Adjusted GDP Per Capita	92
5B.2	Underground Classical Business Cycle Reference Dates: Real Seasonally Adjusted Domestic Product Per Capita	93
5B.3	Comparing Turning Points in the Legitimate and Underground Sectors Using Real Per Capita Measures (1966-96)	93
5B.4	Underground Business Cycle Responses to Cyclical Swings in the Legitimate Economy with a Symmetric Response Model	97

5B.5	Underground Business Cycle Responses to Positive and Negative Shocks in Legitimate Economic Activity	99
5B.6	Testing Whether Negative Shocks have Steeper Effects than Positive Shocks on Underground Economic Activity	100
5C.1	Estimates of the Underground Economy in Australia (1967-96)	102
6.1	Benchmark Financial Ratios for Various Industries	108
6.2	Estimation Results	113
6.3	Effects on the Cash Economy from Changes to Average Taxes and Welfare Benefits	123
6.4	Businesses by Industry: Broad and Fine	126
6.5	Ranking Business and Consumer Contributions to the Cash Economy in Australia	128
6.6	Ranking State's Contributions to the Cash Economy in Australia	130
6A.1	Dickey-Fuller Unit Root Tests	133
6A.2	Endogeniety Tests	134
6A.3	Properties of Residuals	134
6B.1	Estimates of the Cash Economy in Australia – Business and Households	136
7.1	Examples of Identified Welfare Fraud	141
7.2	Informal Economy Report: Recommendations	143
7.3	New Zealand's Compliance Improvement Initiatives	147
7.4	Canada's Compliance Strategy	150
7.5	Selected Cases of Tax Evasion	151
7.6	Housing Construction Industry Initiative	153
7.7	Self-Regulation in the Clothing Industry	164

Preface

When I set out to write this book, my objective was to investigate and measure the extent of distortions in the national accounts arising as a consequence of the Cash Economy in Australia. I was quite alarmed by the results. By the end of October 1999 some 11.5 million Australians completed their tax return, each signing the document to be 'true and correct to the best of their knowledge' but oddly enough some $76 billion went unreported from the Australian Taxation Office (ATO) suggesting that many of these income tax returns were misleading. These findings have a serious implication for the quality of national accounts data collected by the statistician as well as for the implementation of government policy.

Although my motivations for writing this book were to examine these distortions, it very quickly took many new directions. With an econometric approach to estimating its size, I examined a number of separate issues including the effects of tax evasion on government revenue, the impacts of the new tax system on underground activity, the characteristics of the participants engaging in the cash economy and in particular the industries more prone to become involved. I believe this book makes an important contribution in understanding the dynamics and consequences of illicit behaviour in Australia, and that you as the reader will find the results to be quite interesting, and possibly surprising.

Christopher Bajada

Sydney, Australia.

Acknowledgements

I wish to thank the following for their helpful comments throughout the various stages that this book has undergone: Ross Milbourne, Graham Voss, Neil Warren, Glenn Otto and Joao Ricardo Faria. The final product has been much enriched by their efforts and I am grateful to them all.

List of Abbreviations

ABN	Australian Business Number
ABS	Australian Bureau of Statistics
ANA	Australian National Accounts
ATM	Automatic Teller Machine
ATO	Australian Taxation Office
BAS	Business Activity Statement
CETF	Cash Economy Task Force
EFTPOS	Electronic Funds Transfer at Point of Sale
GST	Goods and Service Tax
HST	Harmonized Sales Tax
PAYE	Pay-As-You-Earn
PAYG	Pay-As-You-Go
PPS	Prescribed Payments System
PST	Provincial Sales Tax
RBA	Reserve Bank of Australia
RPS	Reportable Payment System
VAT	Value Added Tax

1 Introduction

At some stage many of us have discussed amongst friends and colleagues our view of the amount of income we forgo to the government in the form of taxes and the government's use of these tax collections to fund public works. Typically the discussion results in a unanimous agreement that tax collections are excessive and could be better distributed amongst the various public works that the government has committed itself to providing. As one thing leads to another, tax evasion and avoidance become the topic of attention. If we are particularly unhappy with the government's handling of the public purse, we may be more supportive of tax evasion and avoidance than we would be if we perceived the government was using public funds in an appropriate and efficient manner. Although these perceptions will turn out to be quite important in determining participation in the 'underground economy', it is necessary that we identify, at the outset, the distinction between tax evasion and avoidance. We will argue that tax evasion will form part of the underground economy and tax avoidance will not. Loosely defined, the underground economy may be interpreted as unmeasured economic activity that has contributed to value, as defined by the national accounts, but goes unmeasured by society's current measurement techniques. The underground economy has been variously described as illicit, cash, irregular, black, shadow, parallel, subterranean, dual, clandestine, gray, moonlight, submerged or hidden activities.

Tax avoidance typically involves a lawful arrangement by the taxpayer to take the necessary steps to minimize their tax obligations by taking advantage of a loophole in the tax system. For example, a taxpayer can reduce their tax obligations by making charitable contributions or by taking full advantage of all taxable deductions. Tax evasion on the other hand is unlawful. It usually involves overstating expenses, claiming expenses that were never made, under-reporting income or simply not reporting income at all. While legal tax avoidance does not distort the quality of the national accounts, tax evasion leads to significant downward bias. If we are interested in improving the quality of the national accounts, we need to have some idea of the extent of tax evasion that is actually taking place in the economy and to take the appropriate steps to do something about it. The principle objective of this book is to provide an estimate of the size of the underground economy (or tax evasion) in Australia and to come to understand the motives that are driving the participation. In this way it may be possible to make some suggestions to help combat, what anecdotal evidence suggests, is a growing underground economy in Australia.

Times may be tough but many ordinary Australians are doing it better than they will admit. By the end of October 1999, some 11.5 million Australians completed their annual tax return, each signing the document to be 'true and correct' to the best of their knowledge. Households account for 85% of total taxpayers while companies and partnerships account for 5% and 4% respectively.[1] Oddly enough since 1995 some $78 billion has gone unreported annually from the Australian Taxation Office (ATO) suggesting many of these income tax returns were in fact misleading. A back-of-an-envelope calculation would suggest that the household sector alone is evading approximately $10 billion in tax liabilities that adds about $1100 annually to the tax liability of the honest taxpayer given current participation in the underground economy.

As a percentage of GDP, the underground economy in Australia has shown strong signs of resilience to government attempts to curb back its size. Measuring on average about 15% of GDP since the mid-to-late 1960s suggests that not only are many ordinary Australians cheating the government from tax revenue, but it appears that the activities have been entrenched in the working ethics over many years. What is even more disturbing is the fact that many of these tax cheats will remain undetected and will continue to lodge misleading tax returns in the future.

Not only are the actions of the tax cheats reducing the size of the tax base and tax revenue, they also affect the quality of economic data which the Australian Bureau of Statistics collects and which policy makers use to gauge their policies. Can we say that the Australian National Accounts (ANA) portray an accurate measure of the activities that are taking place in the economy? Is the inflation rate representative of the prices Australian households are paying for their goods and services? A large underground economy would suggest the answer to each of these questions is no.

If your neighbour, who by trade is a mechanic, offers to repair your car for a price significantly lower than you would otherwise pay, the offer may be too attractive to turn down. Of course, if you accepted the offer, you would be expected to make the payment in cash. Because cash leaves no trail for the tax office to follow, it provides ample opportunity for your neighbour, and others, to evade their tax obligations. In Economics we refer to the outcome as a *Pareto Improvement*. This means that not only has the mechanic benefited by evading taxes, but you, as the consumer, also benefit from paying a fraction of the price you would otherwise have paid if a legitimate mechanic carried out the repair. Because both parties mutually benefit from the agreement, there is no incentive to report each other to the tax office. However can we say that this is a long-run Pareto Improvement? The answer is probably no because if there are sufficiently large number of agents participating in the underground economy, the impact on tax revenue will most certainly be significant. With commitments and obligations to fund public works, the government may need to increase taxes to compensate for falling revenue. Ultimately the mechanic's tax break will become your tax burden.

But how does this affect the national account statistics? To better understand this, it is necessary to review what the national accounts are attempting to measure. The ANA measures the economic pulse of the Australian economy and provides the basis for formulating policy that attempts to smooth out business cycle fluctuations. In the ANA, the Australian Bureau of Statistics (ABS) estimates the size of economic activity by calculating Gross Domestic Product (GDP). There are three alternative measures by which the ABS calculates GDP:[2] (1) the expenditure approach; (2) the income approach; and (3) the production approach. In principle these three methods should yield the same results but in practice they do not. The ABS statistician is required to introduce a 'Statistical Discrepancy' item in the ANA in order to reconcile the income side with the expenditure side. The expenditure approach, GDP(E), sums the total expenditures taking place in the economy while the income approach, GDP(I), sums the income derived from the production of the goods and services that make up total GDP. Whenever an underground economic transaction is undertaken both the income measure and the expenditure measures are distorted. Suppose we continue with our mechanic example. If the mechanic fails to declare the money received from repairing your car, GDP(I) is that much lower. On the other hand neither is your expenditure recorded and consequently the GDP(E) is also underestimated. However most underground activities require a combination of labour and physical inputs. The physical inputs are generally purchased in the legitimate economy and recorded in the national accounts. It is the labour services, if they go unreported, that distort the national accounts. The mechanic's use of spare parts, if purchased from the legitimate economy, would be measured in the national accounts, but the labour service fee, if not reported to the ATO, will not be measured.

Although many underground activities are difficult to detect, the ATO has uncovered a number of individuals and businesses concealing income and evading taxes. However the number of detections are too few compared, to what we will later show, to be a large underground economy. The following are some examples the ATO has uncovered:[3]

- A small clothing business did not declare cash payments and only recorded cheque payments. When the ATO audited the books of the clothing business, the taxpayer admitted cash was used to pay for private living expenses and wages to employees (who most probably did not declare their income either). The taxpayer received an amended tax assessment;
- A small gardening business kept two sets of books over a four year period – one for cash receipts and the other for cheques. Although only one book was reported for income tax purposes, the two books were kept because the taxpayer had intentions to sell the business. The second set of books was uncovered by the ATO during an audit. The taxpayer received an amended tax assessment for the entire four years and was prosecuted for making false statements to the tax office;
- A large restaurant business was discovered hiding money by ensuring the cash registers would not record the restaurant's takings for the day. The taxpayer was paying cash wages to the employees. Each employee received a Group Certificate for less than they were actually paid. Neither the business nor the employees declared their actual earnings to the tax office and have consequently received amended tax assessments. Prosecutions are also likely to occur;
- A fruit grower made a private arrangement with their agent for a $1 per carton charge to be invoiced as a special type of delivery charge. The taxpayer would receive from the agent this amount periodically and would pocket the cash. The taxpayer would then use the invoice to claim a tax deduction for the expenses. The taxpayer had their tax assessment amended and received a gaol sentence.

These types of activities are not typical to Australia but occur in many, if not all, countries abroad. In fact the following are some cases that tax offices abroad have detected:

- *Japan*[4] – in 1983 the Japanese National Tax Agency discovered significant tax evasion taking place in the fishing industry. The National Tax Agency discovered that a typically high-income earning fisherman would under-report an average annual salary of a salaried worker. It investigated 243 high-income earners in the fishing industry to find that they had all been cheating. In fact the many luxuries that they owned were beyond their means had they fulfilled their tax obligations. Many of them owned large apartments, yachts, and luxury cars. In another survey of 570 service companies (including software firms) detected 233 of these companies had not declared income to the tax office. On average each of these companies concealed about 75% of that concealed by the average fisherman;
- *United States*[5] – 'Coyotes' (men at border points responsible for smuggling immigrants) smuggle people across the United States border and sell them for a steep fee. The immigrants, who typically end up working on farms, usually pay the 'coyotes' up front or if they do not have enough money, they pay with their labour. However in more recent years these illegal immigrants began moving into urban areas as the number of raids in rural areas increase. Once these workers find themselves in the cities, they take part in a number of underground activities to earn a living. Because they are not legal residents, they are forced to remain in the underground economy permanently. The tax office and immigration officials have detected many illegal immigrants who either were given residency status because of their circumstances or they were deported back to their country of origin;
- *Canada*[6] – A Canadian pub was discovered, during 1994 to 1997, to have made a number of false expenses in an attempt to reduce its taxable income. The pub owner was claiming a large number of complimentary meals as 'promotional expenses' when in fact these meals were being paid for by the patrons in cash. The pub owner was claiming the expenses of providing the meals but concealing the income generated from the sale of these meals. The pub owner has since had his tax assessment adjusted.

There has been much concern recently about the extent of tax evasion and rightly so. After all, the implications are quite serious. First, an underground economy reduces tax revenue that could otherwise be used to fund community services. It also increases the tax burden of the many honest Australians who are complying with their tax obligations. Second, it may encourage honest Australians to participate in the underground economy particularly if they observe tax cheats are constantly eluding the tax authorities of their tax obligations. After all, the benefits are immediate – a larger disposable income and greater opportunities for welfare fraud particularly for those in the lower income brackets.

There appears to be strong anecdotal evidence in Australia to suggest that the underground economy is entrenched in the psyche of many ordinary Australians. It is occasionally typical for a tradesman to offer two prices – one for cash and another for cheque.[7] However to be certain of such anecdotal evidence, many academics have produced various methods to measure the extent of tax evasion in their country and abroad. In Chapter Two we identify an appropriate taxonomy for evaluating these illicit activities and in Chapter Three we discuss the various methodologies to measure the underground economy. We will use the term underground economy to mean all types of tax evasion that takes place in the economy and the 'cash economy' to represent a sub-set of activities in the underground economy which involve cash specific transactions.

Unfortunately the various names, that are synonymously used when discussing the underground economy, portray different images of the sort of activities that may be taking place. The same term could even mean different things to different people. For example, the term *cash economy* may either be interpreted to mean only unmeasured legitimate transactions, or it could include criminal activities, such as drug trafficking or prostitution, that are not measured in the national accounts. Consequently the various expressions and interpretations have produced a spectra of estimates for any one country in any given year. For example, in the United States during 1976, the estimates varied between 3.5% (Tanzi, 1983) and 22% (Feige, 1979) of GNP, while estimates for the United Kingdom during 1979, varied between 2% (O'Higgins, 1981) and 14% (Bhattacharyya, 1990) of GNP. For Sweden the estimates for 1978 varied between 3% (Hansson, 1982) and 15% (Frey and Pommerehne, 1984) of GNP, while for Germany, the estimates were just as variable, ranging between 3% (Kirchgassner, 1981), and 16% (Petersen, 1982) of GNP. More recently Karoleff, Mirus and Smith (1993) estimated the size of the underground economy in Canada to be between 15% and 22% of GDP while Statistics Canada believes the underground economy to be much smaller – between 1% and 5% of GDP. In Figure 1.1 we present the various diverging estimates as a percentage of GDP for the period 1976 to 1980. For each country, the various definitions and methodologies (*to be discussed below*) have produced a wide spectrum of results that, to the casual observer, are quite unconvincing. However, a closer look at each of the methodologies and definitions will serve as the explanation for why the results are what they are.

Figure 1.1   Discrepancies in the Estimates of the Underground Economy Abroad (1976-80)

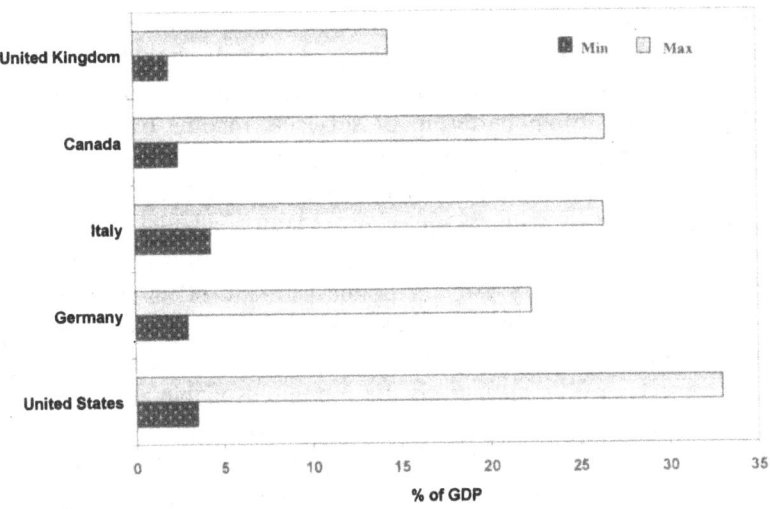

What is the Underground Economy?

It is no surprise that the lack of uniformity in defining the underground economy has produced so many varied estimates of its size. Unfortunately, even today, there is no uniform definition of the underground economy. *Why is this so?* The answer may be as simple as it is complicated – *simple* because some academics are interested in measuring all economic activity, while others are interested only in measuring unreported legitimate activities (activities measured in the national accounts) – and *complicated*, because the many methodologies used are not able to capture the same breadth as intended by the definition, whichever is chosen.

For our purposes we regard the underground economy as consisting of activities which would normally be measured in the national accounts, but because of the failure to report income in whole or in-part is neither measured nor taxed. All forms of criminal activities, such as theft, drug trafficking and prostitution, are generally not part of the underground economy. All types of do-it-yourself activities, such as household repairs and maintenance by the homeowner as well as other non-market activities, do not form part of the underground economy. In principal it is because neither of these activities are measured in the national accounts. Because we are interested only in the extent by which the national accounts are under-estimated, these activities are not included.

Estimating the size of the underground economy is an onerous task. Any serious attempt to measure the underground economy should be able to measure a range of activities. These activities may include income generated from babysitting, bartering of services, income evaded by the mechanic who chooses to report only part of their income, businesses that overstate their expenses, legitimate income earned and laundered abroad, and income concealed by welfare recipients. Many academic studies have simply focused on some aspects of the vast array of underground activities, and in doing so provide only a lower bound estimate of its size. For our purposes we will only be estimating that part of the underground economy that requires the use of cash to settle transactions, that is, the cash economy. As we will argue later, this measure is not too unreasonable an estimate of the underground economy because the other types of activities that are not capture by our estimates are likely to be detected by the ATO. These activities therefore are likely to be limited in number and size. Nevertheless an understanding of these limitations helps to reconcile why the many estimates are so variable even for the same country. In Chapter Three we present the various alternatives employed by academics attempting to estimate the underground economy elsewhere.

Why is it Important?

Particularly in academia, applied economic research generally assumes a greater emphasis on the quantitative approaches to estimation and forecasting and little or no attention to the quality of data used in the estimation processes. To the casual observer the underground economy has a number of important implications. These include:

- Unreliable data affects the credibility of any statistical estimates attempting to model an economic phenomenon;
- It may give rise to inefficient policy prescriptions particularly if it is driven by changes in the published data. The gauge most commonly used to measure the functioning of the economy, namely the behaviour of economic variables, can be significantly distorted by the existence of a non-negligible underground economy and undoubtedly this has a serious implication for the business cycle in general;
- Significant underground activity deprives the government of much needed tax revenue to fund public works;
- Honest businesses face the threat of closure with unfair price competition coming from businesses that actively participate in the underground economy in an attempt to cut costs.

Recently the ATO has undertaken steps towards devoting some of its resources to tackling the underground economy in Australia. In 1996 the Australian Commissioner for Taxation established a Cash Economy Task Force (CETF) to address what appeared to be a growing community perception that the cash economy was growing. In the process much has been learnt on what motivates the participants in the underground economy and these will be dealt with in greater detail in Chapter Four.

Although minimizing tax obligations appears to be the most sensible explanation for participation in the cash economy, numerous other motives have also been suggested. One proposition put forward argues that the cash economy offers an escape from economic hardship in the legitimate economy, allowing individuals to take on additional work which may otherwise not be available in the legitimate economy. If this is in fact true, then such transactions act as an automatic stabilizing mechanism during periods of economic recession, much the same way transfer payments affect the economic cycle. However the findings in Chapter Five suggest that the business cycle of the cash and legitimate economy are procyclical. This simply means that the business cycle of the legitimate and underground economy move together, that is, when the legitimate economy is growing, the underground economy is observed to be growing also. At the same time any downturn in legitimate activity is mirrored by similar declines in underground activity. This finding implies the cash economy is failing as a stabilizing mechanism and to the contrary, increases the volatility of the business cycle in general. That is to say, if we were to adjust the national account statistics by the estimates we obtain for the underground economy, economic growth (or decline) is much larger than what the statistics are actually suggesting. The implications are that policymakers and the market are uninformed about the true state of economic affairs.

A second proposition suggests that the cash economy offers individuals accessibility to goods and services that may not be readily available in the legitimate economy because of inadequate demand. This is somewhat more difficult to assess because prior knowledge of what is being traded in the cash economy is required and such information is simply not available. Typically what we find is that much of the activities taking place in the underground economy is similar, if not the same, to the type of activities taking place in the legitimate economy. Nevertheless, as sensible as this argument may appear, it is quite likely that only a small percentage of participants engage in the cash economy in search of goods not available in the legitimate market. It is more reasonable to expect that participation in the cash economy is driven by participants' attempts to increase their disposable income above levels which would otherwise be possible in the legitimate economy after factoring in the necessary tax obligations.

However since a significant degree of autonomy and freedom, as well as the absence of government taxes and regulation characterize the underground economy, it still remains uncertain how effective government policies will be in reducing illicit behaviour. A number of policies have already been set in motion to curb back illicit behaviour in Australia, particularly in the clothing, textile and footwear, primary production and taxi industries. Preliminary results released by the ATO suggest that their policies have been successful to some extent. For example, the ATO's Compliance Initiative Program returned the government an additional $1-$1.8 billion between 1989 and 1992, while for 1996/7 the figure rose to $2 billion (ATO, 1998a).

Introduction 11

In July 2000, Australia undertook a major step in reforming the taxation system by introducing a Goods and Services Tax (GST). The tax displaced part of the government's tax revenue from direct taxation with an across-the-board tax of 10% on most goods and services. The structural change in tax collections will undoubtedly have an effect on the extent of illicit activities in Australia as it has had in countries that have introduced similar tax reforms. Whether the cash economy shrinks or expands is yet to be seen. One of the themes in this book is to measure the impact the GST has had on the underground economy and to determine who, in the underground economy, has been hardest hit by its introduction - businesses or households?

The Howard government, particularly prior to the changes in the tax system, argued fervently that the new reporting requirement of the GST would ensure that much of the cash economy would be detected and taxed. The government had argued that the GST will increase the tax base and the revenue raised will be used to fund the growing demand for public goods and services. In countries such as Canada, Britain and New Zealand, were similar attempts to reform the tax system have been made, the outcomes have been less than favourable for the government. Not long after each tax reform, there were clear signs in each of these countries that size of the cash economy was growing. Although the Australian tax system shares similar features with those of Canada, New Zealand, and Britain, the Australian government is hoping that the few differences, namely the Australian Business Number (ABN), will ultimately succeed in curbing the cash economy. Public perception in Australia of the effectiveness of the GST in meeting the government's cash economy objectives have been largely influenced by such overwhelming international evidence. In fact public opinion prior to the tax changes were generally unanimous in concluding that the cash economy would increase as a result of the tax change (see BRW, 2000).

Estimates of the Underground Economy in Australia

Implications for Macroeconomic Management

Considerable international literature has been devoted to estimating the size, and investing the consequences of the underground economy. In 1977, Professor Peter Gutmann provided the first published estimate for the

United States and his work generated considerable interest. Those who became interested in the underground economy developed a number of techniques to estimate its size, the details of which are postponed until Chapter Three. Surprisingly no one pursued the cause for Australia and consequently very little is known on the Australian underground economy. Only speculation has provided us with any estimates of its size - roughly 10% of GDP. This book provides the first comprehensive research on this topic for Australia. The findings suggest that not only has the underground economy been a significant part of economic activities, but also production in the underground economy exhibits strong business cycle fluctuations. That is, there are periods when participation in the underground economy grows strongly and periods when participation declines rapidly.

Why is the business cycle so important? The business cycle simply stated is the regular patterns in expansions and recoveries in economic activity around a trend growth path. The role of the policymaker is to monitor such business cycle fluctuations with the intentions of smoothing large swings that may arise from time to time. For example, if the economy is overheating or is steering towards recession, policymakers are expected to enact changes in government policy to manage these swings in order to maintain consumer and business confidence. As information on the business cycle is often gauged from National Accounts data, the quality of these accounts is extremely important for this task. Because the underground economy is not measured in official statistics, policymakers may be unaware of the true extent of economic activities taking place in the economy. Consequently the economy may be overheating or contracting more than the official data suggest. The implications are that policy changes may be inadequate to smooth the true swings in economic activity being generated by the combination of legitimate and underground activity.

A Cashless Society?

Our modern society is becoming more and more dependent on electronic means of payment. If you take note next time you go shopping you will realize that a vast number of consumers are using credit and debit cards to pay for their goods and services. The growth of electronic payments has come about because of the convenience it offers. Goods and services can now be paid for over the telephone, consumers no longer need to make cash withdrawals from their bank before going shopping, and more recently, consumers can redeem points earned on their credit cards for flights

Introduction 13

overseas.[8] The combination of these factors has in recent years reduced our dependence on cash. Although currency is still used everyday to settle quite a large number of small transactions, the proliferation of electronic means of payments suggests a decline in the use of currency will continue.

What do currency statistics suggest? Despite the widespread use of substitutes for currency there has been in the last twenty years a surprisingly large amount of currency outstanding in Australia. Although consumers and firms still use currency to settle everyday transactions, an increasing number of these transactions are being paid for by electronic means. This would suggest that the quantity of cash carried by any person at any one time should be lower on average than ten or fifteen years ago, after adjusting for inflation.[9] In Figure 1.2 we plot the stock of currency in the hands of the public measured in real and in real per capita terms.

Figure 1.2 Measures of Currency – Nominal and Real (1989-90) Per Capita

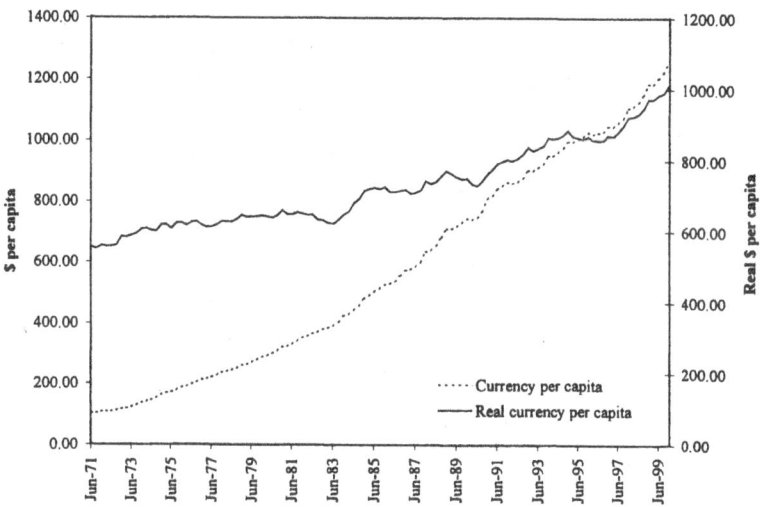

From Figure 1.2 it is clear that despite increasing use of electronic facilities for everyday transactions, the volume of currency in circulation has been increasing quite steadily, particularly in recent years. In December 1990, the stock of currency in the hands of the public was approximately $755 in real per capita terms (or $800 in nominal per capita terms), while in

December 1999, the stock of outstanding currency rose to $1011 in real per capita terms (or $1255 in nominal per capita terms). This is in spite of the fact that EFTPOS, ATMs and other electronic means of payments, such as Visa and American Express, have grown dramatically over this period.

These figures are particularly puzzling at first glance because very few Australians, carry on average $1,000 or more in their wallets. The figure is much larger if adjusted for a population aged 15 and over who are likely to be holding currency. In recent times debit and credit card use has become the norm for retail payments in Australia. In 1999, 43% of all transactions in Australia were made using credit and debit cards (ACCC, 2000). This amounts to 1.2 billion transactions worth $91 billion. Other factors must be at the center of this rapid growth in currency stock and legitimate consumption appears not to be the explanation.

The rapid growth in currency has since left many puzzled, unable to explain how the rapid growth in currency and its substitutes could coincide together. Part of the answer lies in the growth of the underground economy.[10] Cash dominates exchange in the underground economy because it leaves no audit trail, unlike cheques or electronic payments, which do. Knowing that accepting cash payments may conceal tax evasion, the use of cash as a means of exchange will continue to dominate underground transactions in future. The decline in the legitimate use of currency appears to be offset by a growing demand for currency required in support of a growing number of underground transactions.

Plan of this Book

This book provides the first comprehensive discussion of the underground economy in Australia with the intention of addressing three central objectives. Firstly, to understand why a suspiciously large amount of currency remains outstanding and cannot be explained by legitimate transactions alone. Secondly, to examine the factors that motivate individuals to participate in the underground economy and the consequences they may have on the business cycle, on the quality of the National Accounts and on taxation revenue. And finally, our third objective is to examine whether households or businesses are contributing most to the underground economy and whether the new tax system, introduced in July 2000, will have any impact on underground activities in Australia.

In Chapter Two we begin by introducing the various definitions of the underground economy that exist. We adopt the view that the underground economy should measure the unobserved activities that would otherwise be measured by the national accountant and no more. We will show that the various definitions have resulted in a number of estimates that are remarkably different from one another, even for the same country.

Chapter Three elaborates on the methods that have been used to estimate the underground economy abroad. Unfortunately some of the methods which have been used have not encompassed the same breadth as the definition of the underground economy intended, so the results need to be interpreted in context. Chapter Four introduces a discussion of the factors that motivate participation in the underground economy. We argue that although there may be a number of factors motivating participation, increasing disposable income is likely to be the dominating factor. The same chapter introduces a discussion of the consequences that are likely to result from growing non-compliance.

In Chapter Five we estimate the size of the underground economy in Australia. The findings suggest that the underground economy has for many years acted as a haven for significant tax evasion. We discover the underground economy in Australia has business cycle characteristics similar to those of the legitimate economy. The implications, which are also discussed in an appendix to Chapter Five, imply that the true business cycle is much more volatile that national account statistics suggest.

In Chapter Six, the analysis is extended to measure the contributions to the underground economy by businesses and households. A closer look at businesses by industry classification and geographical region helps to produce a ranking of industries according to their participation. In helping to combat the underground economy, Chapter Seven introduces a discussion of the methods that have been used to combat the underground economy abroad. In keeping with the results of Chapters Five and Six, an assessment on the likelihood that such policies could reduce the underground economy in Australia is taken up.

Notes

1   Taxation Statistics 1998-99.
2   Recently the ABS implemented the *System of National Accounts* (SNA93) into the ANA. While significantly contributing to an improvement in the measurement of national output, the changes have only had a small impact on the movement of GDP

(ABS, 1998). The three alternative measures of calculating GDP are no longer explicitly published, replaced now by a single measure. To ensure that the components do balance, the statistical discrepancy is now allocated to each of the components based on information from input-output tables. Although the statistical discrepancy is no longer explicitly reported, an estimate of its size is nevertheless possible to construct.

3   ATO (1997).
4   Seeman (1984).
5   ABS (1990).
6   CCRA (2001c).
7   This was certainly the case before the introduction of the GST. It is too early at this stage to comment on whether such a practice is likely to continue. It certainly may be more feasible for it to continue in the services sector where the uses of inputs into production are quite limited. This will be explored in a later chapter of the book.
8   The Reserve Bank of Australia (RBA) recently has shown some concern for the growth in debt levels amongst Australian consumers. The RBA has attributed a significant part of this growth in debt levels to the 'Frequent Flyer' programs. These programs typically award the consumer one point for every dollar they spend and the consumer can, at a later date, redeem these points for domestic or international travel.
9   Alternatively these results suggest that the velocity of currency should have risen overtime. The velocity measures the number of times the stock of money is turned over annually in financing the annual flow of income. With a smaller stock of money in circulation, the remaining money stock must circulate faster to finance a given flow of income. The velocity of currency has declined very rapidly since 1981 despite of the rapidly growing number of currency substitutes.
10 Although criminal activities are not discussed to any great extent in this book, criminal activities, vis-à-vis money laundering, is another major explanation for why the stock of currency may have risen also.

2 What is the Underground Economy?

An Overview

The underground economy has been written about extensively but its definition has always been a matter of contention. For some authors the underground economy encapsulates activities that ought to be recorded in the national accounts but is not because of taxpayers' failure to report income in whole or in part. For others it includes not only activities that fall within national accounting boundaries but also illegal activities such as prostitution and drug trades. In some countries certain activities, which are illegal by Australian standards, are not illegal. This throws open the possibility for including them in the activities of the underground economy particularly if we argue the national accounting case. Yet again, other authors argue that do-it-yourself and non-market activities should be measured as part of the underground economy. These inconsistencies have undoubtedly led to the vast array of estimates of the underground economy we have seen in Chapter One and cast doubts on their reliability for public policy making. It is the development of the national accounting system that appears to have contributed in some respects to this confusion.

Most countries follow the system of national accounts maintained by the United Nations, particularly because they also provide an economic report of domestic economic conditions to them according to this convention. It also serves as an appropriate way to make international comparisons of economic growth overtime. The first version of that system, announced in 1953, was specifically designed to include all legal and illegal transactions that took place in a given year. However a recent survey of member nations revealed that even with sophisticated statistical systems, including illegal transactions in the national accounts is quite difficult.[1]

The ABS has identified a few factors contributing to measurement deficiencies in GDP.[2] In this book we will limit our concerns to economic activity that is not measured because of tax evasion. The reader may wish to consult Bajada (2001) for a review of the measurement deficiencies of

GDP and their impact on public policy. In summary, the major sources of deficiencies identified by the ABS are quoted as follows. Note that the ABS does not explicitly quote the underground economy as a measurement problem although it acknowledges its consequences.

> The major area of understatement on the income side is considered to be income of unincorporated enterprises, which is difficult to estimate accurately because of understatement of income as reported to the Taxation Commissioner (the major source of data). On the Expenditure side there are three major areas of known understatement because of inadequate data sources, viz.:
>
> i) No estimate has been included of the expenses associated with the sale of dwellings and other buildings and land, e.g. legal fees, real estate commission, stamp duty.
> ii) No estimate has been included in capital expenditure on private dwellings to cover those alterations and additions that either do not require a local government permit or for which the owner does not obtain the requisite permit.
> iii) No estimate is included in private final consumption expenditure for expenditure on illegal goods and services, e.g. no allowance is made for the purchase of illicit drugs or payments relating to illegal gambling and prostitution.

It would appear that although in practice the ABS does not include illegal activities in the measurement of national output, the remark (iii) above would suggest that in principle illegal activities could be included. The reason simply stated is that these activities are 'productive' activities that generate income for those involved and could be subject to taxation. Some countries in keeping with the conventions of the United Nations National Accounting System, report what we regard as illegal activities as part of GDP.

There are of course disadvantages of omitting illegal activities from the national accounts. For example, the US constitutional amendment in 1932, which repealed the prohibition on alcoholic beverages set in place during 1920, had an impact on the growth rate for that period. Of course such circumstances not only make it difficult to have a consistent time series of national accounts data for any one particular country, but there is a greater difficulty in making international comparisons when different countries have different legal systems. For example, drug use and prostitution are illegal in Australia, while in some European countries they are not.[3] The reader may wish to refer to Carson (1984a) and Blades (1983) for further details.

How does this affect our discussion of the underground economy? The answer is extremely important because it could mean the difference between an estimate of the underground economy that is small, and another that is large. The Australian National Accounts provides regular estimates of GDP which measure the value of final goods and services produced in a given year. It excludes illegal activities such as drug trafficking, prostitution, laundering of money, illegal gambling, selected pornography, smuggling and loan sharking. The production of current goods and services reported in the national accounts are generally taxed and the revenue used to fund government's public works programs. Illegal activities on the other hand are prohibited and do not contribute to tax revenue.

So if we are interested in the extent of tax evasion, we should only concern ourselves with those activities that are taxable. This implies that illegal activities should not be included in the measurement of the underground economy in Australia. Countries that include some of the activities that we regard illegal should in principal include these in their measure of the underground economy. So it is more important that we define the underground economy in terms of unmeasured national output rather than in terms of selected activities that may or may not be illegal in some countries.

For choice of a better word we will use criminal activities to define those activities that are prohibited by law, excluded from the national accounts and not subject to taxation. We will use the term illegal activities to define those underground activities that would otherwise form part of the national accounts and taxed but are not because of failure to disclose the relevant income. We separate hard-core criminal activities from criminal activities because the latter produces an income to the offender while the former is typically characterized by physical violence, for example, murder or rape.

Although we have presented the argument why the underground economy should not include illegal activities, Smith (1997) summarizes the various interpretations of the underground economy that are found in the literature. They include:

- Defining underground economic activity as unmeasured activity that falls within the production boundaries of the national accounts;
- Including what would normally be measured in the national accounts *plus* criminal activities;

- Including what would normally be measured in the national accounts *plus* criminal, non-market and do-it-yourself activities.[4]

Let us take each of these in turn.

Consistency with National Accounts

There are numerous types of activities that would be measured in the ANA but because of failure to report income in whole or in-part does not get measured. Many economists have adopted the view that only activities measured in the national accounts should be regarded as activities taking place in the underground economy. The following are some of the examples consistent with this definition.

- *Moonlighting/misleading tax returns* A waitress, who decides to take on some additional part-time work on the weekend, seeks employment with a local catering business. The employer agrees to employ the young waitress on a cash wage basis. The waitress willingly accepts the offer knowing that cash presents her with the best means to avoid complying with her income tax obligations. It may also mean that the employer could offer the employee a lower wage, in an attempt to reduce costs, knowing that the employee could nevertheless still be better off avoiding income tax. On the other hand, her employer does not have to contribute to superannuation, pay payroll tax and comply with industrial relations laws that generally add to the costs of legitimate employment. The outcome is likely to give the employer a competitive advantage over honest competitors in the industry;
- *Professional services* which are generally provided outside normal working hours. Examples include motor vehicles repairs, hairdressing, painting and decorating, plumbing services, accounting and financial services. Some of these services may have their 'value' separated into two components – the value of materials used and the value of services rendered. It is most often the case for these type of underground activities, that materials purchased will have been obtained and paid for in the legitimate economy and therefore recorded in official statistics. It is the value of the service however, if it goes unreported, that becomes part of the underground economy. This is termed as the value added to the

material purchased in the legitimate economy and is subject to our investigation;
- *Tax relief* received by self-employed for expenditures that could otherwise be classified as legitimate consumption expenditure not necessarily connected with the running expenses of a business also forms part of our measure of the underground economy. Examples may include the reporting of private functions (or celebrations) as a business function so that the taxpayer reports a larger than actual business expenditure in an attempt to reduce the firm's tax liability;
- *Welfare benefit fraud* Individuals in receipt of unemployment benefits (or any other form of welfare relief) may actively work for cash and not disclosing this income because it may affect their entitlement to these benefits. For example, an unemployed writer who takes on some work editing manuscripts conceals this income so that it would not affect his or her unemployment benefits. However a strong possibility exists that even though this person finds a more permanent job, the activity may continue indefinitely. Although this would not necessarily constitute welfare fraud, it may mean that those receiving benefits while in transition between jobs may be lured into the underground economy. Its attractiveness may then mean that the illicit activity could continue indefinitely reducing the government's tax revenue. Other types of welfare fraud may be more intentional particularly by those who intend to stay on welfare benefits and to undertake odd jobs to improve their financial position that may otherwise be less favourable if they are normally employed in a low-income profession;
- Failing to declare interest income or dividend payments;
- *Barter* The exchange of services from one professional to another. For example an electrician may exchange their services in return for the services offered by a plumber. This may also include the payment of services in kind;
- *Concealing rent* For example, a retired couple transforms their garage to an unregistered 'granny flat' so that they may supplement their pension with a small rental income. To conceal this from the tax authorities they find a tenant without employing a real estate agent.

Including Criminal Activities

Feige (1996) provides a taxonomic framework for classifying the various types of underground activities. In this framework the underground economy is defined to include not only the activities that are measured in the national accounts but also criminal activities. The four types of underground activities identified by Feige are:

- *Illegal (criminal) activities* The production and distribution of these 'goods or services' are a criminal and punishable offence. The manufacturing and sale of drugs is an example of an illegal activity. The extent of illegal activities are generally measured by crime statistics and in Australia the evidence suggests that these activities have grown significantly over the last ten years. For Australia the total cost of abuse of illicit drugs (including loss of productivity, property crime and damage) during 1988 was approximately $1,200 million (see Collins & Lapsley, 1991). The incidence of drug use and related break and enters have since risen dramatically and governments are more frequently discussing public policies to control drug-use and drug-related crimes. Other types of illegal activities include (1) *insurance fraud*: the Insurance Council of Australia (1992) estimated insurance fraud to be approximately $1,700 million annually; (2) *computer abuses*: Schramn (1990) suggests that fraudulent use of credit cards, banking facilities and other forms of computer abuses range between $300 and $700 million; and (3) *theft*: Instances where an employee fraudulently under-reports a firm's income in order to increase their own disposable income is a criminal action and is not measured in the activities of the underground economy. Quite simply this is a redistribution of income from the firm to the employee (by theft) and contributes nothing to value added. Only if the employer and employee are in cahoots can we regard this as an activity of the underground economy. Potas et. al (1990) estimates for Australia, based on insurance payouts, that motor vehicle theft alone costs over $650 million annually;
- *Unreported activities* Although these transactions are subject to taxation, individuals fail to report this income to the ATO in an attempt to increase their disposable income. A monetary measure of the extent of unreported activities is given by the net tax gap.

The net tax gap measures the difference between potential tax revenue and the amount actually paid while the gross tax gap measures the difference between potential tax revenue that is legally due to the government and tax revenue that is voluntarily paid. The difference between the gross and the net figures represents the volume of tax paid as a result of direct enforcement by the taxation office. Without an appropriate educational strategy to teach the general populace of the costs of tax evasion and strategies to combat growing non-compliance, this difference is more than likely to be quite small. Because welfare benefit also has an implication for tax revenue, welfare benefit fraud is also included in the measure of the tax gap;

- *Unrecorded activities* These activities are economic activities that circumvent the institutional rules that define the reporting requirements of government statistical agents (Feige, 1996). A measure of these unrecorded activities may be gauged by measuring the difference between the income that should be recorded in the national accounts and that income which is actually reported;
- *Informal activities* These activities are those which circumvent the legal and administrative rules, covering property, commercial licensing, financial credit, and labour contracts, in an attempt to either reduces costs or to increase benefits.

Including Criminal and Non-market Activities

The perspective on what constitutes underground economic activity is very broad. It encompasses not only what would normally be measured in the national accounts but also activities that are not. The activities that are not measured in the national accounts include all forms of criminal, non-market and do-it-yourself activities (see Pozo, 1996a). We have already defined what constitutes criminal activities, so enough said on this. Non-market activities include a vast array of activities that do not always generate income and do not contribute to the income tax base.[5] Non-market activities include rent on owner occupied dwellings,[6] food consumed on farms, and income in kind given to religious members of the community. Do-it-yourself activities include a vast array of house bound activities such as growing of fruit and vegetables for private consumption, repairs to home, car, and TV by the owner, gardening, general housework such as painting and decorating as well as cleaning.

In Table 2.1 below we identify some of the many studies that have taken the various views of the underground economy as they have been portrayed above. Although many have taken the *Consistency with National Accounts* approach, there are sufficient numbers of others that have not and which have undoubtedly contributed to the vast array of estimates of the underground economy that we have seen in Chapter One and will see in Chapter Three.

A Re-stated Taxonomy of the Underground Economy

Feige (1996) goes beyond the activities that are measured in the national accounts by introducing illegal activities, such as drug trafficking. It is our view that this is inappropriate because we are interested specifically in activities, which, if unreported, distort the national accounts, and reduce the government's tax revenue. Although the extent of drug trafficking, for example, is important to know in its own right, it is not measured in the national accounts and nor does it contribute the government's tax revenue in Australia. For this very reason we separate these activities from the underground economy. For the same reason we exclude non-market transactions and do-it-yourself activities.

Table 2.1 Defining the Underground Economy

Consistency with the National Accounts	Including Crime	Including Non-Market and Do-it-yourself Activities
Bhattacharyya (1990)	Gutmann (1977)	Reed (1985)
Frey & Weck-Hannemann (1984)	Macafee (1980)	CBA (1980)
Tanzi (1980, 1983)	Porter and Bayer (1989)	Hill (1979)
Van Eck & Kazemier (1988)	Mirus, Smith & Karoleff (1994)	Gershuny (1979)
Feige (1979)		
Frey, Weck & Pommerehne (1982)		
Cox (1984)		

What is the Underground Economy? 25

To begin with, we introduce a simplification to this taxonomy consistent with the scope of the CETF whose objective it is to try to understand the size and nature of the 'cash' economy in Australia. This revised taxonomy of economic activities is presented in Figure 2.1 below and complements much of the most recent literature on the topic (see Williams and Windebank, 1995; Schneider, 1997; and Kaufmann, Johnson and Zoido-Lobaton, 1998).

Figure 2.1   A Modified Taxonomy of Economic Activities

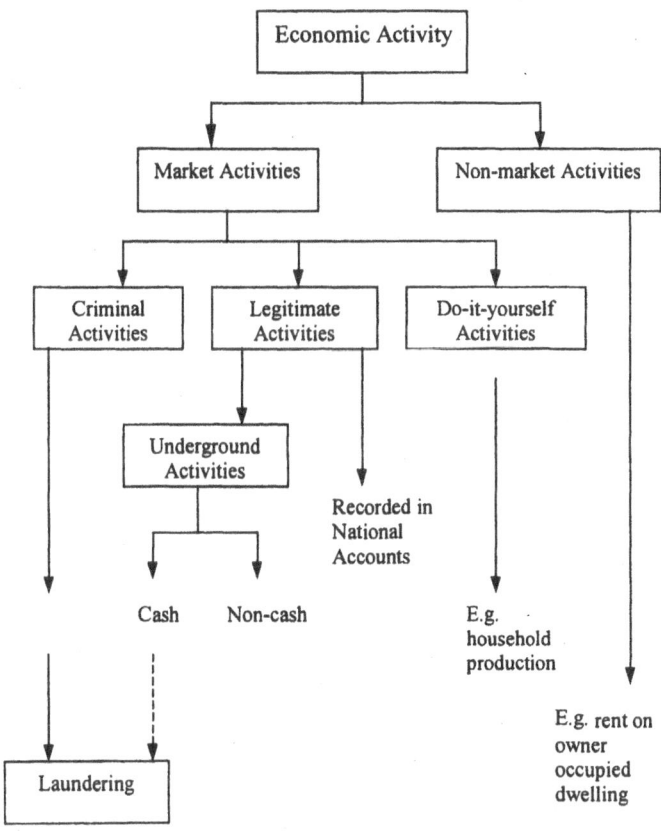

Figure 2.1 classifies the various types of economic activities taking place in the economy. These activities may fall into either one of the following two broad categories: Market and Non-market Activities. The market activities can be classified into a further three categories which include criminal, legitimate and do-it-yourself activities. Legitimate activities include all those activities that would normally be measured in the national accounts and are generally taxable activities. Most transactions in Australia and abroad are predominantly legitimate activities. However some of these activities go unreported. We regard all these unreported activities as constituting our measure of the underground economy. Increasing disposable income is predominantly the major force motivating individuals or businesses to conceal income from the tax office. These unreported transaction impacts on the quality of the national accounts and on the effectiveness of public policy, which is driven by the release of data in these accounts.

Being able to estimate the volume of these unreported transactions produces some obvious benefits. First, the government may appropriately gauge the cost of compliance initiatives against the likelihood of revenue that may be netted from the underground economy.[7] This is only feasible if the extent of tax evasion is known. Second, policy makers are in a better position to know the extent of changes in economic fundamentals that may not be obvious or adequately measured by national accounts data.

The characteristic of these unreported (underground) activities allows for a dual classification - those that involve cash transactions and those that do not. The example of the mechanic given in Chapter One is typical of unreported activities involving a cash transaction, while failing to declare interest income or overstating business expenditures are underground activities that do not involve the use of cash. This distinction is important because the methodology that will be used in Chapter Five, (and used in others: see Giles, 1999b; and Schneider 1999), produces estimates of cash transactions in the underground economy. Consequently the estimates presented in Chapter Five should be regarded as a lower bound estimate of the underground economy. However non-cash transactions are likely to leave an audit trail for the tax office to pursue, unlike cash transactions that do not. Therefore those non-cash transactions are likely to be a very small component of the underground economy because of this strong possibility of detection.

Since we are interested only in unreported activities that distort the national accounts, criminal activities are excluded from our measure of the underground economy in Australia. Typically governments are interested in eliminating criminal activity not taxing it. Including criminal activities will only produce misleading expectation of potential tax revenue from any successful tax compliance initiative. In Figure 2.1 criminal activities are represented as a separate component of economic activity. Our methodology for estimating the cash economy in Australia is capable of distinguishing between cash earnings from criminal activities and cash earnings from legitimate activities.

Similarly, do-it-yourself activities are distinctively different from activities of the underground economy. These activities are generally excluded from the national accounts because of the difficulty in quantifying the market value of production and the problem of data collection. Consequently these activities do not constitute part of the tax base and are represented as a separate component of market activities. Although these too understate the extent of GDP, they are generally accepted, unlike underground activities, as unavoidable measurement problems that most countries have had to be content with. Non-market activities on the other hand typically do not generate an income and in Figure 2.1 are represented as distinct from market activities.

Although in Figure 2.1 we introduce the possibility of money laundering, we do not take up the topic here. Although money laundering may be a channel to conceal earnings from the underground economy, it would be more appropriately dealt with in a book of its own. We need to appreciate however the possibility that earnings from either criminal or underground activities could be laundered abroad to avoid detection by local government authorities. In Figure 2.1, two arrows, one solid and the other dashed, identify the income source of laundering. The solid line represents a strong flow while the dashed line, a much weaker flow. It is reasonable to expect a greater volume of money laundering takes place from income generated by criminal activity rather than from underground activity. In Chapter Six we provide some evidence why we might expect this to be true.

Notes

1. Blades, D. (1982), The Hidden Economy and the National Accounts, *Occasional Studies, Organization for Economic Cooperation and Development*, June, pp. 28-45.
2. Australian Bureau of Statistics (ABS) (1990), *Australian National Accounts – Concepts Sources and Methods*, Canberra, AGPS, pp. 158-59.
3. See Blades, D. (1983), Crime: What Should Be Included in the National Accounts and What Difference Would It Make? Presented at the International Conference on 'The Economics of the Shadow Economy', University of Bielefeld, October 10-14.
4. Occasionally this alternative may only include non-market and do-it-yourself activities.
5. See Carson (1984a).
6. This is an imputed calculation in the ANA.
7. This would be significantly distorted if criminal and non-market activities were included in the estimate of the underground economy.

3 Methodologies for Estimating the Underground Economy

There appears to be a number of broad categories into which the attempts to measure the underground economy fall. Although each approach differs from application to application, the underlying conclusions from the majority of these studies are that the underground economy worldwide has been growing over time. Our objective is to review these methodologies and to identify the advantages or disadvantages of each. These methodologies may be grouped loosely as follows:

Voluntary Survey and Samples

Using this approach for estimating the size of the underground economy, individuals are interviewed and asked whether they have actively participated in the underground economy. Some surveys take the form of direct contact between the interviewer and the respondents selected for the survey. In other surveys the respondents are requested to complete a questionnaire and to mail back their responses. Other surveys use combinations of the two methods for eliciting information. Typically the questions may specifically ask the respondent if they acted as a buyer or seller in the underground economy. Others may use more indirect questioning in an attempt to overcome the bias in responses that result from directly asking the respondent whether they have failed to meet their tax obligations.

Although susceptible to significant bias from the sensitive nature of the topic (Hansson, 1989), surveys have typically been favoured by government departments interested to know the extent of illicit economic behaviour. Typically surveys are in the form of interviews in which a representative sample of the population is asked whether they have participated as buyers or sellers of labour and/or goods in the underground economy. Surveys from Italy (Censis, 1976), the United States (Ross, 1978), Britain (Dilnot and Morris, 1981), Belgium (Pestiau, 1983), Norway

(Isachsen and Strom, 1989), Netherlands (Van Eck and Kazemier, 1988), and Germany (Frey, Weck and Pommerehne, 1982), each reached the conclusion that the extent of illicit economic behaviour has been growing over time and was likely to continue to do so in the future.

Although such surveys have the potential to uncover detailed information about the quality of work and the characteristics of employment (see Frey and Pommerehne, 1984), it is doubtful whether in fact such techniques have the potential to uncover most of the underground activities taking place at any one time. For example, in a Norwegian postal survey Isachsen, Klovland and Strom (1982) found that more people admitted to paying for irregular services than actually participating in the underground economy. Similarly in Australia, the Australian Taxation Office found the general public perceived underground activities to be widespread while small business believed the trend to be declining. Therefore because surveys present the possibility of conflicting results they are generally not favoured when attempting to estimate the size of underground economic activities. Although Mogensen, Kvist, Kormendi and Pedersen (1995) use the approach to estimate the size of the underground economy in Denmark, they also discuss the advantages and disadvantages of the use of these techniques to estimate illicit activities.

Non-Voluntary Tax Auditing

Unlike the voluntary nature of surveys, a tax auditing approach is a non-voluntary method by which the tax authorities may uncover concealed income earned by those participating in irregular activities. This approach, as with voluntary surveys, has been used extensively in many countries to detect subterranean activities: the United States (Simon and Witte, 1982), Sweden (Frey and Pommerehne, 1984), United Kingdom (IRS, 1979; and O'Higgins, 1989), Holland (Kinsey, 1987), and France (OECD, 1980).

Using a non-voluntary tax auditing approach for estimating the size of the underground economy has the advantage of unveiling information on the classes of individuals based on occupation who participate in under-reporting their incomes (Koopmans, 1994). This has been of particular interest to the ATO because it allows the tax authorities to concentrate their resources on particular industries: (i) building and construction; (ii) wholesale markets for fruits and vegetables; (iii) road transport including the taxi industry; (iv) clothing manufacturers; (v) restaurants and cafes; and (vi) the computer industry.

However the method of non-voluntary tax auditing is probably more important in identifying over-estimation of deductible expenses rather than under-reporting of income because expenses require receipts and concealed earnings need to be proven (OECD, 1978). As a result only a small part of the underground economy is probably captured using this approach. This small proportion includes those who work and pay some of their tax obligations. It excludes all those who do not work and who are still actively supplying their labour services in the underground economy. It is unlikely that this approach will give reliable information about the true trend of non-compliance over time as the procedure is susceptible and sensitive to changes in tax structure, tax legislation and methods of auditing. Nevertheless this approach is more likely to uncover a larger proportion of the underground economy than those that would be detected based on the voluntary responses of samples and surveys, particularly if individuals fear being punished if detected concealing income (Mirus, Smith and Karoleff, 1994). See also Thomas (1992) for a detailed discussion of fiscal auditing and the implications for measuring illicit activities.

Using the National Accounts

This method relies on a 'residual' approach rather than the direct approach of surveys and tax audits. The method assumes than concealed income will find its way back into the legitimate economy in the form of legitimately measured expenditure. The difference between legitimate income and expenditure may be used to proxy the extent of underground activities (see Matthews, 1984; and Macafee, 1980). This discrepancy approach can be applied at the national or at the household level. At the national level O'Higgins (1981) for the United Kingdom and Macafee (1980) for the United States found rising trends in this discrepancy and concluded that the underground economy was growing. Park (1979) and Hansson (1982) found no such trend for Sweden, and for Germany, Langfelt (1989) found the underground economy to be declining between 1961 and 1974. At the household level, the methodology is somewhat similar but the focus is on disaggregate measures in the discrepancy between income and expenditure. Similarly Yoo and Hyun (1998) use micro-level data to produce estimates of the underground economy in a number of countries.

Irrespective of whether we adopt a national or household approach, a major criticism of this methodology is that the estimates of the size of the underground economy depend on the differences between income and expenditure which are most likely themselves to be affected in measurement by the very existence of the underground economy (Macafee, 1980). Furthermore, there are always errors in the national accounts which are often associated with data collection and processing, as well as the problem of timely collections (ABS, 1990), which as a consequence may further significantly distort any estimate of such subterranean activities. For this reason we do not use the statistical discrepancy as an indicator variable of the size of the underground economy in Australia.

Labour Market

This approach focuses on official labour market statistics in an attempt to estimate the size of the underground economy. However many of the approaches used share a common set of fallacies and so should all be treated with caution. The approach used to measure the size of the underground economy in Italy demonstrates how unreliable these estimates are (Frey and Pommerehne, 1984). In order to measure the size of the irregular workforce it was assumed that it could be calculated as the difference between the participation rate given by official statistics and the participation rate derived from a comparator country or a previously preferred participation rate. The problems of this approach are numerous: (i) the participation rate of a comparator country may itself be affected by a sizeable underground economy; (ii) the participation rate of a comparator country may be influenced by many other factors which are not relevant to the country concerned; (iii) people can work in both the legitimate and underground economies and (iv) it is doubtful when using a benchmark period that the participation rate may be assumed constant over time. Similar problems afflicted the German (Langfelt, 1989), Swedish (Myrsten, 1989), Italian (Contini, 1981), United States (O'Neill, 1983) and Canadian, (Mirus and Smith, 1989) estimates of the underground economy and for this reason they have been unpopular approaches.

Large Bills

This technique of estimating the size of the underground economy is founded on a measure related to the growth of large denominations of currency. Since underground economic transactions are presumed to be settled in cash, an increase in the proportion of currency is required to support a growing underground economy. Therefore it is hypothesised that the growth of the underground economy may be approximated by the growth of large denomination bills, for example, the growth of $100 bills (see Carter, 1984 and Matthews, 1982).

This argument, while interesting, is often misleading as it must control for the effects of inflation. For example, O'Higgins (1989) suggested that while inflation not only has a nominal effect on currency holdings, it also has a substitution effect, that is, individuals do not increase the number of bills they hold for transactions purposes to counteract inflation, they simply substitute smaller denominations for larger ones. Primarily the main reason why the large bills hypothesis has been rejected is that inflation causes what were once large denomination bills to become small denomination bills. This means that the definition of large currency denominations must involve a 'jump' at the point where previous denominations changes from large to small. O'Higgins (1989) found that the large bills method was not an appropriate means by which to approximate the growth or size of the underground economy. The findings were also mirrored in Canada (Mirus and Smith, 1989) and in the United States (Porter and Bayer, 1989). Thus we now turn to estimations based on an alternative, more popular, 'monetary' methodology.

'Monetary Methods'

A very popular methodology to estimating the size of the underground economy are the so-called 'monetary methods' (see Gutmann, 1977; Tanzi, 1983; and Feige, 1979, 1986, 1989). Because those who work in the underground economy make every attempt to remain unobserved from the authorities by explicitly requesting cash as payment for their services, 'monetary' approaches seem to suggest an efficient way to uncover the trail of these participants.

This led to a new 'generation' of models that made every effort to identify the 'extra' currency that may be attributed to the factors which may explain the size of the underground economy. The advantage of this methodology is that it permits an evaluation of, and the change in, the size of the underground economy which may be attributed to the burden of taxation, presumed to be the major factor driving such illicit activities (Frey and Pommerehne, 1984). In Chapter Five we illustrate that such a methodology may also be helpful in identifying the sensitivity of the size of the underground economy from changes in welfare benefits. A 'generous' welfare system may encourage a greater dependence on social security and active participation in underground activities. For this reason the 'monetary' approach is an attractive alternative to measuring the size of the underground economy in Australia.

There have however been various approaches that fall under the heading of 'monetary' methods that we briefly discuss for completeness. The most popular, and the method which we employ with modification in Chapter Five, is the so-called 'Tanzi approach'. Tanzi (1980, 1983), who argued that the main motive for working in the underground economy was to avoid paying taxes, proposed a currency demand approach to estimating the size of the underground economy in the United States. The approach was based on Cagan's (1958) findings that the demand for currency depends on demand deposits, the ratio of personal income tax to personal income and per capita real income. We demonstrate that our modified methodology works well for Australia and provides some very interesting results. The 'Tanzi approach' has recently been used to provide estimates for a number of countries (see Schneider, 1997 and Williams and Windebank, 1995).

The less popular methods have been proposed by Gutmann (1977) and Feige (1979, 1986, 1989) primarily due to their restrictive assumptions and the sensitivity of the estimates to changes in these assumptions. Gutmann (1977) provided the first estimate of the underground economy for the United States by focusing on the growth of the two components forming M1, namely, currency and demand-deposits. In his analysis, Gutmann (1977) assumed that the currency/demand-deposit ratio of 1937-41 was 'normal', that is, there was no underground economy during this period. This approach came under severe criticism, namely because, (i) the currency/demand-deposit ratio approach is highly sensitive to the base year chosen, and (ii) other factors than the growth of the underground economy were driving the currency/demand-deposit ratio, notably the fall in demand-deposits (Garcia, 1978).

Feige (1979) proposed an alternative approach to measuring the underground economy based on the quantity equation of money, $MV = PY$. According to Feige, if it is possible to obtain independent estimates of MV and PY, the difference would represent a measure of the total volume of unrecorded transactions. Assuming 1939 as the year in which there was no underground economy, Feige estimated the size of the illicit activities in the

United States to be 22% and 33% of official GNP for 1976 and 1979 respectively. These results were treated with scepticism particularly when other estimates were less than half of those estimated by Feige (Frey and Pommerehne, 1984) - [see Table 3.1]. Frey and Pommerehne (1984) disbelieved these estimates because (i) the approach produced negative estimates for the underground economy between 1939 and 1968, and (ii) the choice of base year significantly altered the estimates.

Other Methods

There are several other approaches which have been used to estimate the size of the underground economy. Frey, Weck and Pommerehne (1982) suggested a so-called 'soft modelling' approach. In this approach, the factors likely to contribute to the size of the underground economy are assigned weights according to what is perceived to contribute most to the size of illicit activities. These include the burden of taxes and regulation, tax moral index (of individual attitudes towards the government) and the length of the working week. Different weights applied to all the determinants were varied to emphasise the important influences they have on the underground economy. It was found that in Sweden and Norway, taxation and regulation were significant factors contributing to illicit economic activities while for the United States and Canada taxes and regulation were not as dominant as was the rate of unemployment. The problem with this approach is that the estimates are dependent on an arbitrary assignment of weights.

Bhattacharyya (1990) proposed an alternative approach for estimating the underground economy, namely the use of a RESET procedure on a specification of currency demand similar to the optimal cash balance proposition of Baumol and Tobin (1989). For the United Kingdom, Bhattacharyya's (1990) results compared with others proved very mixed. Bhattacharyya estimates the size of the UK underground economy in 1979 at 10.2% of GNP while Barthelemy (1988) estimates it at 14.5%. Macafee (1980) produced much smaller estimates, ranging between 2.5% and 3% of GNP consistent with 2.3% to 3% of GNP by Dilnot and Morris (1981).

Giles (1999c) advocated a latent variable/MIMIC (Multiple Indicator, Multiple Cause) approach to estimating the size of the underground economy in New Zealand. The latent variable model when calibrated with information from a currency demand model was used to produce a historical time series of subterranean activity. The size of the underground economy in New Zealand was found to be between 6.8% and 11.3% of measured GDP. From this, the total tax gap was found to be in order of 6.4% to 10.2% of total tax liability in New Zealand.

Another approach used to estimate the size of the underground economy has become known as the Kauffman (*Physical Input*) method (see Kaufmann and Kaliberda, 1996 and Kaufmann, Johnson and Shleifer, 1997). It assumes that electricity consumption is the best physical input measure of overall economic activity and employs the general empirical result that the elasticity ratio for electricity/GDP is approximately one in many countries. The approach treats this result as the benchmark and measures how each country varies from this general empirical finding. The growth in the underground economy is then assumed to be equal to the difference between the benchmark growth rate (elasticity ratio equal to one) and the actual measure for a particular country. Obviously there are numerous problems with such an approach including: (i) technological improvements change the nature of electricity consumption, (ii) not all underground economic activity requires electricity consumption; and (iii) there are several cross-country differences in the electricity/GDP ratios (see Schneider and Enste, 2000).

Alternatively another technique which may be classed as a Physical Input approach has become known as the Lacko Method (see Lacko, 1996, 1998, 1999). The focus is more specifically on household consumption of electricity in determining the extent of underground economic activities. There are clearly a number of deficiencies in this approach: (i) it assumes that the activities taking place in the underground economy are originating from the household sector and there is no business sector contribution, (ii) the approach encapsulates household production and do-it-yourself activities which we have argued should not be included in the measure of the underground economy, and (iii) not all underground activities require the use of electricity.

In Table 3.1 we present some of the many studies and methodologies which have been used to estimate the size of the underground economy. Every attempt has been made to provide estimates for the late 1970s to enable a suitable comparison of the alternative methodologies. We have also incorporate estimates by Schneider and Enste (2000) for the late 1970s using a number of techniques for a number of countries. It appears that the results are very mixed whichever approach is considered. For example, the transactions approach during the late 1970s estimated the size of the underground economy in Germany to be between 8% and 16% of GNP while the monetary methods produced much smaller estimates, between 2% and 8% of GNP.

Table 3.1 Underground Economy – Methodology and Estimates

Study	Methodology	Country/Time Period	Size of Underground Economy (% of GNP)
Schneider and Enste (2000)	Survey	Canada/1981-85	1.3%
		Germany/1970-75	3.6%
		US/1976-80	4.5%
		UK/1976-80	1.5%
Frey and Pommerehne (1984)	Tax Audit	Sweden/1978	8-15%
O'Higgins (1989)	Tax Audit	UK/1979	9.69-12.9%
Schneider and Enste (2000)	Tax Audit	Italy/1976-80	3.9%
		US/1976-80	6.3%
Carl and Witte (1982)	Tax Audit	US/1972	9-16%
O'Higgins (1981)	Discrepancy	UK/1970	1%
		UK/1974	2%
		UK/1978	2.9%
Macafee (1980)	Discrepancy	UK/1978	3-5%

Study	Methodology	Country/Time Period	Size of Underground Economy (% of GNP)
Hansson (1982)	Discrepancy	Sweden/1970s	3-5%
Schneider and Enste (2000)	Discrepancy	Germany/1976-80	10.2%
		UK/1976-80	3.6%
		Italy/1976-80	4.3%
		US/1976-80	4.9%
Langfelt (1989)	Discrepancy	Germany/1961	16.7%
		Germany/1968	12.6%
		Germany/1974	4.8%
Dilnot and Morris (1981)	Discrepancy	UK/1977	2.3-3%
Smith, Pissarides and Webber (1986)	Discrepancy	UK/1982	5% of GDP
Petersen (1982)	Discrepancy	Germany/1961	16% of GDP
		Germany/1974	4.8% of GDP
Myrsten (1989)	Labour Market	Sweden/1974	15% of official working hours
Schneider and Enste (2000)	Labour Market	Germany/1976-80	38.5%
		Italy/1976-80	18.4%
Mirus and Smith (1989)	Labour Market	Canada/1971	5.6% *
		Canada/1975	14.3% *
		Canada/1982	32.4% *

* = potential supply of hrs/wk over 1970 level

Methodologies 39

Study	Methodology	Country/ Time Period	Size of Underground Economy (% of GNP)
Feige (1979)	Monetary (Transaction)	US/1976 US/1979	22% 33%
Barthelemy (1988)	Monetary (Transaction)	Germany/1969 Germany/1975 Germany/1979	14% of GDP 16% of GDP 24% of GDP
Barthelemy (1988)	Monetary (Transaction)	UK/1969 UK/1975 UK/1979	11% of GDP 14% of GDP 14.5% of GDP
Schneider and Enste (2000)	Monetary (Transaction)	Canada/1976-80 Germany/1976-80 UK/1976-80 Italy/1976-80 US/1976-80	26.5% 22.3% 12.6% 26.4% 24.9%
Langfeldt (1982)	Monetary (Transaction)	Germany/1961 Germany/1974	3% of GDP 8% of GDP
Gutmann (1977)	Monetary	US/1976 US/1979	11% 13.5%
CBA (1980)	Monetary	Australia/1978	10.7% of GDP
Tanzi (1983)	Monetary	US/1976 US/1979	3.56-5.49% 3.71-5.4%
Kirchgassner (1981)	Monetary	Germany/1960 Germany/1970 Germany/1978	2% 3.1% 8%

Study	Methodology	Country/Time Period	Size of Underground Economy (% of GNP)
Schneider and Enste (2000)	Monetary	Canada/1976-80	6.3%
		Germany/1976-80	7.8%
		UK/1976-80	7.9%
		Italy/1976-80	13.2%
		US/1976-80	4.6%
Bhattacharyya (1990)	Monetary	UK/1967	4.89%
		UK/1974	9.25%
		UK/1984	7.92%

4 Motivations and Consequences

When an individual participates in the cash economy and does not pay their fair share of tax, the rest of the community must bear the burden of higher taxes that may be needed to continue funding government expenditure. If there are only a small number of participants in these clandestine activities, the burden may be spread thinly on the community, diluting significantly any adverse effects on those complying with their tax obligations. If on the other hand, the numbers of participants are large and the extent of evasion is significant, the compliant community suffers. As we will see in the following chapter many complying Australian's are shouldering a heavy burden for those who choose not to comply with their tax obligations.

The underground economy is sometimes suggested to offer an escape from the troubling times in the legitimate economy, allowing individuals to stretch their incomes beyond which they could otherwise. It may also offer individuals goods and services that may not be readily available in the legitimate economy because of inadequate demand (Henry, 1981). Generally however, a consensus on this issue of participation advances the viewpoint that individuals engage in underground economic activity in search of greater disposable income. The literature has provided a more comprehensive list of determinants. The first part of this chapter will take a closer look at each of these.

Naturally, once participation takes effect there are a number of consequences that may arise and that may need to be addressed sooner than later. In order to assess the importance of policy in combating growing non-compliance, it is important that we have a thorough understanding of consequences that may arise from active participation in the underground economy. The second half of this chapter will deal specifically with these consequences.

Motivations

Developing strategies to detect tax evasion has been high on the government's agenda for some time now but little effort appears to have been spent coming to terms with what motivates individuals and businesses to engage in underground activity. This apparent lack of interest perhaps signals a poor understanding of such motives. Why should we be interested in what motivates participation in the underground economy? Simply stated, a poor understanding of these motives will limit the success of policies aimed at reducing non-compliant behaviour. In this chapter we illustrate that those who participate in illicit activities are motivated by many factors that are often intertwined. Although we list each of the factors separately, it is important to remember that a number of these factors may be affecting participation simultaneously.

We divide the motives into two categories - those that are institutional and those that are economic. The institutional motives, which include the public's perception of the government and its regulatory environment tend not to change over time even as economic conditions change. These motives may produce the 'persistence' in participation even when attempts are made to reduce such activities. The economic motives, which include the burden of taxes, the rate of inflation, the rate of unemployment, and the extent of welfare benefits, change with changes in economic conditions. The institutional motives may be discouraged by an education campaign, but the economic motives are best dealt with by more effective enforcement. Chapter Seven will take up this discussion.

The *economic factors*, which tend to change over time, include:

Tax Burden

The progressive income tax system is most often regarded as the major economic impediment to fostering a harder work ethic.[1] A second job does not benefit from a tax-free threshold as does the first, and is consequently taxed as though it was additional earnings from the taxpayer's principal occupation. Consequently those who are inclined to take on additional work often do so by moonlighting. This would involve under-reporting or failing to report an income from a second job that is usually paid in cash.

In July 2000, the Howard government introduced a GST as part of its tax reform package. The Howard government advocated that the implementation of the GST and the ABN would, if not eliminate, reduce the underground economy significantly. The evidence in the following chapter suggests the government was wrong in claiming such a successful outcome. The evidence also bears a resemblance to a study by Hill and

Kabir (1996) that finds substituting direct for indirect taxes is not likely to improve tax compliance.

There was much resentment during the early stages of the GST proposal by certain sections of the community, although others including businesses welcomed the changes. However sentiments have since changed. Small businesses in particular have lobbied the government for changes to the reporting requirements which they have argued has added enormous costs to their operations, restricted cash flows and forced a number of small business closures. The government has only recently responded to these cries by simplifying the reporting requirements, although many businesses have argued that the simplifications have not gone far enough.[2] Unfortunately some businesses may have sought relief by participating in the underground economy and may lock in their participation because of the financial benefits that the underground economy has to offer.

In a recent survey of Australian taxpayers, Taylor (2000) finds a large number of respondents bereaving the inequity of the Australian tax system. One quarter of those surveyed expressed the view that the GST is an inequitable tax and the beneficiaries of such a tax system are the wealthy. Similar results were found for Canada (see Flexman, 1997). Asked to comment on the following question:

To what extent, if any, do you feel that people are evading some of their full share of taxes?

more than 60% of Canadian respondents surveyed expressed their concern that there was a lot of evasion amongst Canadian taxpayers.[3] For the following question:

Would most people cheat on their taxes if they knew they could get away with it?

72% of respondents agreed that many Canadian taxpayers would renege on their commitment to meet their tax liabilities if the opportunity became available. The low tax morality amongst Canadian taxpayers would suggest there is a fine line between the decision to work in the legitimate economy or in the underground economy. Unfortunately, there is a 'ratchet effect' in the underground labour market. Those who have participated in the underground economy and enjoyed the benefits of tax-free income would be reluctant to cease participation unless threatened by detection and penalty.

A large part of the literature supposes that the willingness of individuals to avoid the payment of taxes is the principal motivation to participation in the underground economy. The progressive income tax system, which taxes heavily incentives to work hard, may foster an attitude that working in the underground economy is acceptable. When individuals contemplate working in the underground economy, they weigh up their income tax obligations had they worked in the legitimate economy, against the potential earnings for those same hours had they worked in the underground economy, plus any benefits they may earn if they were, for example, unemployed. The following demonstrates the point. An individual who may earn $20 an hour in a legitimate occupation and pays an average tax of say 25%, receives an after tax income of $15 an hour. If the same individual chooses not report this income to the tax office, the person's after tax income is an average of $18 an hour, which assumes a 20% probability of being caught and if caught, paying twice the amount of tax that would normally be paid. If the individual is in search of a larger disposable income, that person appears much better off concealing this income from the tax authorities.

A number of studies have also confirmed what the earlier surveys have found to be the common attitude of taxpayers towards the income tax system. Schneider (1994b) tested a number of variables affecting participation that included the burden of taxation, the complexity of the tax system and the intensity of government regulation. Of the three, the tax burden was the dominant motive affecting participation, followed by the intensity of government regulation and the complexity of the tax system. Similar results were found for Germany (see Kirchgaessner, 1983), Denmark (see Schneider, 1986) and for Norway and Sweden (see Klovland, 1984). Loayza (1996) using a Multiple Indicator, Multiple Cause (MIMIC) model for fourteen Latin American countries, finds that the tax burden and restrictions in the labour market play a major role in encouraging participation in the underground economy.

Unemployment

When economic conditions worsen, unemployment typically rises. In Australia unemployment has been quite high, particularly in recent years and appears quite resilient (at least downwards) to changes in economic conditions. When this unemployed labour finds no alternative avenue for employment it may resurface as clandestine employment. Typically this occurs in response to two factors:

1. Unemployment benefits may not be adequate to sustain the quality of life previously enjoyed by those who have suddenly become unemployed. If a tight labour market limits the opportunity for these people to find new employment, they may be encouraged to participate in the underground economy. Although such employment may be perceived at the outset as transitory, the fact that such activity greatly increases disposable income may entrench the activity even after legitimate employment is found.
2. Those who have become unemployed or employed part-time face increases in disposable time and greater opportunity to pursue employment in the underground economy (see De Gijsel, 1984 and Riebel, 1984). Federal Awards and State legislation prescribe the number of hours an employee is expected to work for an employer. In Australia the standard working week varies from 35 to 40 hours depending on the industry. The shorter the working week the greater are the opportunities for those to take on clandestine employment (see Hunt, 1999; and Lemieux, Fortin and Frechette, 1994).

A combination of the tax structure and unemployment benefits can affect the cyclical behaviour of the underground economy. In turn this could then affect the cyclical behaviour of the legitimate economy and adversely affect policy decisions. For example, the progressive tax system implies that as income increases tax payments increase faster than before. If the increases in taxes change the risk preferences of individuals towards tax evasion, the effect could mean a greater participation in the underground economy. If this happens a cyclical upswing in the legitimate economy produces a similar upswing in underground activity implying the two cycles are pro-cyclical. However if the underground economy is an avenue of refuge during periods of economic decline, the business cycles of the legitimate and underground economies are counter-cyclical. That is, economic activity in the underground economy picks up when opportunities in the legitimate economy decline. In the next chapter we will test which of the two effects dominate. The result is extremely important because if the two cycles are pro-cyclical to one another the true business cycle is more volatile than known to policymakers. If, on the other hand, the two are counter-cyclical, the underground economy is smoothing volatility in legitimate activity and may in fact be assisting policymakers in smoothing economic fluctuations.

Inflation

Inflationary pressures have an adverse effect on the purchasing power of income, and unless wages are indexed to inflation, real disposable income falls. For example, a couple on a fixed nominal income faced with a 6% inflation rate, will experience a 6% fall in the real purchasing power of their income. Those who are receiving unemployment benefits, usually fixed in nominal terms over a given period, are faced with the same constraints as inflation rises. To compensate for this adverse effect, there may be strong incentives to work in the underground economy (O'Higgins, 1985; and CBA, 1980).

Typically prices in the underground economy are set on the basis of prices in the legitimate sector. Generally one would expect to see that when prices increase in legitimate economy, similar price increases are expected to occur in the underground economy. Inflationary pressures can therefore make working in the underground economy more appealing and increase the nominal volume of tax evasion taking place. By evading taxes, those participating in the underground economy also increase their tax savings because they avoid the harmful effects of bracket creep. The combination of the larger tax saving and nominal income the underground economy offers may even encourage new participants. If we believe that a person's exposure to the benefits of participating in the underground economy make it unappealing to leave, it is important that inflationary pressures are closely monitored.

Generous Unemployment Benefits

For others, the combinations of untaxed income and welfare benefits may foster welfare dependence particularly if the combined earnings are in excess of the lower income entitlement from the legitimate economy. Workers in receipt of unemployment benefits may be discouraged from participating in the legitimate workforce when there is the possibility of greater disposable income from the combination of welfare benefits and clandestine activities. Under such circumstances generous welfare benefits may continue to foster growth in the underground economy (see also Frey and Weck-Hannemann, 1984).

Welfare dependence is determined to a large extent by the recipient's attitude towards work, by the amount of the payment received in proportion to the award wage, and by the possibility of employment in the underground economy. Unlike countries that have limited or no social security for those who become unemployed, Australia has a relatively generous welfare system. Unfortunately some abuse the privilege by claiming to be unsuccessful in finding employment, while others find employment in the underground economy but remain officially 'unemployed' to retain their 'entitlement' to welfare payments. In particular, low-income earners engaging in underground activity, while receiving unemployment benefits, may earn more than from legitimate employment. Therefore any increases in unemployment benefits as a proportion of household disposable income can only trigger more participation in the underground economy.

Cost Cutting by Firms

Financial security is a major concern for small businesses and more often than not it hinges on the firm's ability to price-compete with other small firms in its industry. Effective price competitiveness may be possible by sub-contracting work in the underground economy so as to reduce costs. With cheaper costs of production the firm is able to secure a larger market share by lowering its price at the expense of legitimate businesses. Such unfair price competition may lead to many small business closures.

Friends and/or Relatives

Another motive for participating in the underground economy is an individual's knowledge that friends and/or relatives are engaged in these activities. Knowing that friends and/or relatives are under-reporting or failing to report income and consistently eluding authorities may motivate others to participate (see Cowell, 1990). This may entrench attitudes in the community that clandestine activities are acceptable and keep the size of the underground economy at persistently high levels.

The institutional motives, which tend not to change over time and which may be contributing to the persistently large underground economy in Australia, include:

Attitude towards Government

A more frequently advocated defense for participating in the underground economy is that the government is a corrupt body that more often spends its revenue from taxes in ways that are inefficient and not in the best interest of the community. Often perceptions of the government are driven by a particular policy or even the perception that the government is not capable of limiting the growth of tax evasion (see Carson, 1984). Growing cynicism and disillusionment particularly by those who cannot find legitimate employment or who perceive widespread abuse of the welfare benefits scheme, may change their perceptions on fulfilling their own tax obligations. Knowing or being advised to take advantage of loopholes that may exists in the tax system not only encourages tax avoidance but may also change an individual's perception on tax morality in general. Unfortunately if perceptions do change then without question participation in the underground economy will increase.

Frey, Weck and Pommerehne (1982) found from a survey of German taxpayers that since 1960 approval of tax evasion rose consistently. The ATO (1997) came across similar evidence amongst Australian taxpayers and has subsequently implemented a number of strategies to encourage voluntary compliance and deter participation in the underground economy (the details can be found in Chapter Seven). In another survey, US taxpayers were questioned on their perceptions of government and income taxes. Using questions such as:

> *Do you consider the amount of Federal income taxes which you have to pay is too high?*
>
> *Do you think that the government wastes a lot of money?*
>
> *Do you think that the government is untrustworthy?*
>
> *Do you think that the government does not care much about what people like you think?*

the survey results helped produce an index to determine whether over time tax morality has shifted away towards non-compliance. Using 1970 as the base year, the following results were published:

Table 4.1 Tax Morality Index (Germany)

	1960	1965	1970	1975	1978
Index	62	73	100	118	121

Source: Frey & Weck-Hannemann (1984).

These results suggest that over the period from 1960 to 1978 tax morality in the US had declined significantly, consistent with the findings at the time that the underground economy in the US had also grown.

Probability of Audits

An individual's decision to participate in the underground economy is often driven by perceived probabilities of detection. If the perceived probability of an audit is high, particularly if it is public knowledge that the tax office is targeting certain occupations, participation may decline. However perceptions are unlikely to change with changes in economic conditions. This implies that if the probability of being detected is regarded to be low, participation in the underground economy could well persist over time, if not increase.

Generally most taxpayers are risk averse and as long as they perceive the probability of detection to be quite small, they are unlikely to participate in the underground economy. However in the face of financial constraints an individual may accept a greater risk in an attempt to alleviate their financial burden. For example a policy that increases taxes not only reduces after-tax income but it may also encourage individuals to take on additional risk to compensate the fall in their disposable income (see Houston, 1987). That is, there may be a positive relationship between acceptable risk and participation. Of course participation may decline if the risk, or the probability of detection increases (see Cebula, 1997).

Government Regulations

Regulations come in many forms including minimum wages regulation, working conditions, hours worked and overtime paid, environmental safety, minimum age laws, work safety conditions, certifications for trades and professions such as plumbers, electricians, bricklayers, doctors, lawyers, and dentists, and regulations governing child care and nursing homes. If regulations either limit income earnings, the conditions under which employees are employed or adds to the costs of production in general, it could inspire participation in the underground economy. For example, health and safety procedures that may often involve much bureaucratic time to approve are often ignored in any production undertaken in the underground economy (see Gaetani-d'Aragona, 1981). Although attempting to quantify regulations and test their impact on the underground economy may be difficult, Frey, Weck and Pommerehne (1982) do provide one method by which to approach its measurement. The procedure involves a direct attempt by comparing general performance under two different conditions, one under regulation and another without. As an example they compare the highly regulated US railroads with the less regulated Canadian railroads. The cost of regulation is then assessed on the performances of these two scenarios. The second approach is an indirect attempt to measure regulation using an indicator of regulatory intensity. This measure is constructed as the sum of regulation for a base year that is given an index of 100. A series is then constructed based on this index as the number of regulations change. They find that an increase in the burden of regulation promotes activity in the underground economy.

Consequences

> *What if the thermometer reads 104 °F when the patient's real temperature is 98.6 °F, and what if the thermometer reads 98.6 °F when the real temperature is 104 °F?* (Greenfield, 1993).

The underground economy serves as the vehicle by which economic agents escape the inspections and regulations of government. It is also the same vehicle that creates economic 'anarchy' to the extent that it undermines 'the stability and responsibility of political, legal and economic institutions that might otherwise serve to facilitate the (economic) development process' (Priest, 1994). An analysis of the underground economy is incomplete without discussing its consequences on legitimate economic activity. Whichever motive fosters active participation, the consequences of a large underground economy may turn out to be quite significant. For this reason it is important to improve our understanding of these consequences to help identify strategies to discourage clandestine activities. The consequences may be summarized as follows.

Declining Taxation Revenue

The overwhelming interest in the cash economy is with the extent of uncollected tax revenue. Although this is not the only serious consequence of tax evasion, it nevertheless warrants significant attention. Whenever participation in the cash economy expands, tax revenue losses add to the financial pressures of government to satisfy the service needs of the community. Daunted with spending decisions and commitments the government, in response to falls in revenue, may either cut its expenditures, raise taxes or finance its expenditures by running larger deficits. Doing so may drive more individuals into the underground economy or encourage existing underground participants to work more extensively (Carter, 1984). The effect may be further compounded as higher taxes reduce investment and savings, inhibiting the growth of the legitimate economy.

We will illustrate in the next chapter that the size of the tax gap in Australia - the size of the tax revenue that is foregone as a result of the underground economy - has been has been growing in recent years. In fact the Australian government has foregone an average of $10 billion annually since 1991 in the form of tax evasion. This implies that a successful initiative to target the cash economy may provide great scope for significant increases in revenue for the government. Conservative estimates for Canada have shown that the Canadian government is losing an average of $6 billion annually in tax revenue from the cash economy (Berger, 1986). Estimates for New Zealand portray the same scenario. Estimates suggest that the New Zealand government is loosing between 6.4% and 10.2% of total tax liability from the cash economy (Giles, 1999b).

Distortions of Economic and Social Data

Individuals and businesses that participate in the cash economy not only contribute to lower levels of tax revenue, but they also bias economic and social information which policymakers use to gauge their economic policies. The fact that the cash economy in Australia will be shown to be quite large by overseas standards suggests national accounts information in Australia is significantly under-estimated. Immediately this distorts measures of economic growth (Houston, 1990), the rate of inflation (Reuter, 1982), the size of the business cycle (to be discussed in Chapter Five), the rate of unemployment (McDonald, 1984), productivity (Carson, 1984), the size of the tax base (Hansson, 1982), and the volume of savings (Greenfield, 1993). Incorrect policy prescriptions can only follow from such data distortions. For example, the fact the unemployment may be consistently upward biased because of the underground economy may result in policies that are too expansionary and generate inflationary pressures.

Tax Morality

If the community acknowledges that the cash economy is growing and not being detected, there is an incentive to encourage a more active involvement or motivate new participants to join. Unfortunately the incentives that encourage a participant to join usually have to be followed by strong deterrence policies to have them quit. Generally once a participant crosses over to the underground economy it may be quite difficult to bring them back, particularly since the financial gains to those who participate are immediate.

Unfair Price Competition

By its very nature, the cash economy promotes unfair price competition. If a business sub-contracts labour from the cash economy at significantly lower costs, the firm is in a better position to price compete with its competitors, who may not participate in the cash economy. Alternatively the firm may engage in selling goods and services in the cash economy while concealing all or part of its income. Unfortunately active participation in the cash economy may force some small legitimate businesses out of the market or force their survival by driving them to participate also.

Welfare Effects

Those who participate in the cash economy may be contributing far less than honest taxpayers for the rights to use government goods and services. The government provides a vast array of goods and services including law enforcement, defense, education, hospitals, roadwork, transport and emergency services. In order that these services may be provided, it is expected that everybody pays their fair share of taxes. If there are a large number of individuals who are participating in the underground economy and not paying their fair share of tax, yet continue to expect the provision of public goods and services, they burden honest tax payers with the burden of raising the finances for their provision. As long as illicit activities are growing, the resource flow from the legitimate to the cash economy implies significant welfare losses.

The competitive advantage that the cash economy offers without doubt contributes considerably to efficiency and productivity losses (see Hansson, 1982). A growth in the underground economy may mean the closure of a large number of small businesses. Recently in Australia the number of small business closures has increased alarmingly. Although the GST and the mild economic climate may explain this trend, the growth in the underground economy would, without doubt, have had some impact on these outcomes.

Implications for Efficiency

The underground economy may distort the allocation of economic resources particularly if it channels them into sectors of the economy where tax evasion is more pronounced. The inefficiencies may become larger if the inefficient redistribution of resources impacts on the methods of production, for example, changing to small-scale production techniques, employing fewer workers, fewer tools and equipment and less specialization (see Kesselman, 1997). There may also be further implications for efficiency if decisions to consume or invest are distorted as a consequence. Kesselman (1997) argues that individuals who participate in the underground economy are more likely to increase their consumption rather than their savings or expenditure on consumer durables because doing so would attract the tax administration's attention. They may even invest very small amounts of human capital in their underground employment in fear that it may only have a short lifespan.

Unregulated Activities

There is also the inevitable consequence of poor work place practices in the underground economy. Goods and services that are provided in the underground economy do not offer the same guarantees of workmanship as one would expect of goods and services provided in the legitimate sector. Unfortunately there are many goods and services that are provided in the legitimate economy under strict health and safety guidelines which ensure adequate consumer protection. However goods and services provided in the underground economy are unlikely to conform in the same way to these guidelines. For example, hairdressers operating legitimately are expected to meet health and safety standards as prescribed in their code of practice. Yet the same hairdresser operating from their backyard after hours may ignore these rules and regulations particularly if it adds to their costs or limits the time the participant has to earn an income in the underground economy. Other examples may include poor plumping and electrical services that may produce significant costs in repairs or pose a fire risk to the occupants.

Income Distribution

Those who are presently on a low income could increase their disposable income by working in the cash economy and claiming to be unemployed in order to receive welfare assistance. The combined income could in most cases exceed the wage received for similar (low paid) work in legitimate economy. The flow of welfare benefits to those who are actively engaged in clandestine activities implies not only an inefficient redistribution of income, but it may also imply that measures of income inequality may be far from what the official statistics suggest (Skolka, 1984).

Benefits?

Needless to say, there are also some benefits that have been advocated as a consequence of the cash economy. A notable remark by a former Italian Prime Minister highlights the point:

> *It is a bad thing to say, but these 'deviations' are a positive thing, at least as far as employment is concerned. If the taxman was to intervene in the underground economy he would be acting in accordance with the principles of distributive justice but would be ruining not only a host of small businessmen and their workers, but perhaps the country's economy and social peace as well* (De Grazia, 1982).

With the exception of employment a number of others have suggested potential benefits that may accrue from an underground economy. These include:

- Portes et al. (1989) suggests that the cash economy may adapt faster to changes in economic conditions thereby helping to accelerate structural changes necessary for economic development;
- Skolka (1984) has suggested that the underground economy may generate positive welfare effects by redistributing income;
- Prager (1983) has credited the underground economy with the provision of goods that may not otherwise be available in the legitimate economy. Such a statement may be true of less developed economies that may have deficient planning for reallocating resources (Carter, 1984). However for the more developed countries this proposition is unlikely to hold;
- Harding and Jenkins (1989) argue that not only does the cash economy foster competition, it reduces pressure on wages, stimulating economic growth while keeping inflation low;
- Operators that have a monopolistic control on the market for the goods and services that they provide, may be made more efficient in the production and distribution as a consequence of those who are operating in the underground economy in the same market for their goods and services (Kesselman, 1997).

As appealing as these may sound, the efficiency gains may only be small and insignificant to outweigh the costs from non-compliance described earlier. There appears to be no evidence at all to suggest that the underground economy does foster structural change that may take place in the legitimate economy. In fact evidence from audits suggest that there is nothing innovative in the underground economy. The activities found to operate in the underground economy are very similar, if not identical, to those occupations found in the legitimate economy. Neither is there any evidence that the underground economy promotes competition. It appears that there are more disadvantages from having a sizeable underground economy than there can be from any benefits that it may have to offer.

Notes

[1] See Tanzi (1980, 1982); CBA (1980); Frey and Weck (1983); Greenfield (1993); Frey and Weck-Hannemann (1984); Carson (1984); Frey and Pommerehne (1984); Ziberfarb (1986); Thomas (1992); Pozo (1996); Giles (1999); Schneider (1994a, 1997, 1998a, 1999) and Schneider and Enste (2000).

2   The reporting requirement changes apply to businesses with an annual turnover of $1 million or less.
3   The survey question could not distinguish between taxpayer's understanding of illegal tax evasion and legal tax avoidance.

5 Estimating the Size of the Underground Economy for Australia

Up until the late 1970s, academics and public officials paid very little scholarly attention to the size of illicit economic behaviour that may be taking place. Gutmann (1977) provided the first published estimate of the size of the underground economy in the United States and his work subsequently generated considerable interest.[1] Much of this interest focused on the size of subterranean activities in several countries other than for Australia. CBA (1980) and Carter (1984) have discussed illicit economic behaviour in Australia however neither of these studies has provided a time series estimate of its size that could be used to gauge the extent of tax evasion taking place in Australia.[2] Many of the consequences that we will allude to in this and in Chapter Six have ignited fresh concerns about how to deal with the underground economy. In fact governments around the world are beginning to increase the amount of financial resources they have previously devoted to tackling the underground economy.

In Chapter Two the underground economy was defined to contain a subset of activities that are principally supported by cash payments. We distinguished these activities by referring to them as taking place in the cash economy. We also argued that there exists other forms of tax evasion that do not involve the use of currency but because they are likely to leave an audit trail they might only represent a small part of the underground economy. In this and in the following chapter we present the most comprehensive estimates of the Australian cash economy to date. In this chapter we develop a model to help determine the extent of illicit activities that are taking place in Australia and in Chapter Six we take a closer look at these estimates to determine who in the Australian economy is contributing most to these illicit activities. These results are important for helping design policies to target activities in the underground economy and can assist policy makers in identifying high-risk areas of non-compliance that may require more urgent attention.

It makes perfect sense to begin our discussion of the cash economy in Australia by taking a closer look at the volume of currency in circulation. Since the early 1960s, the stock of currency in circulation in Australia has grown consistently, particularly since the early 1980s. Much of this growth has been the result of a growing population base and increases in consumption associated with increases in living standards. However what is most puzzling is the fact the real currency per capita grew more rapidly since the introduction of electronic substitutes such as debit and credit cards and other forms of electronic funds transfers (see Figure 1.2).

The factors that determine the use of currency may be gauged from the taxonomy of activities presented in Figure 2.1. From this figure there are three factors that are driving the growth of currency stock, namely, the growth in legitimate, underground and criminal activities. Legitimate household consumption expenditure in Australia has grown an average 3.5% annually over the last 10 years. Although currency supports much of this consumption expenditure, the rapid growth in currency substitutes in recent years has offset much of the demand for currency that we previously would have observed. The implications are clear – something other than legitimate consumption expenditure must be explaining the growing demand for currency. This leaves only criminal activities and the underground economy.

In recent years there has been a rapid growth in crime throughout Australia, evident in statistics collected by the National Crime Authority. Drug trafficking, prostitution and the sale of other prohibited and stolen goods are predominantly settled in cash. A growth in these activities is tantamount to a growth in the use of currency. Similarly, anecdotal evidence and ATO surveys have found that the cash economy in Australia is growing and without question this adds to demand for currency. For this reason it makes goods sense to approach the method of estimating the size of the cash economy by examining the money supply for clues to its size.

Methodology

By convention an individual's real demand for money at time t is expressed as a function of the prevailing rate of interest and the individual's planned spending during that period (see Pagan & Volker, 1981). This can expressed as:

$$M = f(Y, R) \tag{5.1}$$

where M measures the real demand for money (which typically consists of currency and demand deposits). f denotes a mathematical function; Y denotes income and R denotes the interest rate. This model typically produces f increasing in Y and decreasing in R. In other words, as income (Y) increases the demand for money increases as consumption expenditure increases. Interest rates, R, represent an opportunity cost of holding money. Because holding money pays no interest, as R increases the demand for currency is expected to decline.

Because currency forms a sub-set of money (M) we may expect the demand for currency to depend similarly on the level of income and interest rates. Our approach to estimating the size of the cash economy takes account of other explanatory variables that may be driving currency demand. Since the tax burden and welfare benefit payments may encourage participation in the cash economy, it makes sense to incorporate these (and others) into the model. The demand for currency may also depend on the rate of inflation.[3] Rising rates of inflation, for example, erode the value of money and induce individuals to hold less of it. Similarly we may add private consumption expenditure as a percentage of GDP to capture currency demand arising as a result of spending on goods and services (derived demand) in the legitimate economy by underground participants that would not normally be captured by the measure of disposable income. Finally, technological development in the financial sector has no doubt changed the means by which we pay for goods and services and we use a trend variable to capture such technological developments.[4]

Therefore we need to begin with a new specification of currency demand unlike (5.1) above. With an appropriate model for currency demand we estimate the size of the cash economy by looking at the excess sensitivity *(to be discussed below)* of real currency holdings per capita to average tax rates[5] and government welfare benefits. Since the methodology we employ to estimate the size of the underground economy requires the measurement of the excess sensitivity of taxes and welfare benefits on currency, we need to use disposable income rather than income as an explanatory variable. This will be particularly important in our analysis because it may mean that overseas studies, which have used a similar approach, have potentially under-estimated the size of the underground economy.[6]

We can summarize this new model in the following specification for currency demand:

$$C = f(YD, R, \pi, E, Tr) \tag{5.2}$$

where
C = real currency per capita where currency is defined as the total stock of notes and coins in the hands of the public;
YD = real disposable income per capita where disposable income is calculated as income accruing to persons, enterprises and organizations (Y) less total direct taxation (Tx) plus welfare benefits (Wf);
R = the interest rate;
π = the rate of inflation;
E = private consumption expenditure as a percentage of GDP;
Tr = technological trend variable.

In this formulation, taxation and welfare benefits will affect currency through disposable income, since (5.2) could alternatively be written as:

$$C = f(Y - Tx + Wf, R, \pi, E, Tr) \qquad (5.2a)$$

However, it is the *excess* sensitivity of Tx and Wf on currency in which we are interested; that is, whether changes in taxes and welfare benefits changes currency holdings in addition to the affects on disposable income. Thus we consider the estimation of currency demand as:

$$C = f(Y - Tx + Wf, R, \pi, E, Tx, Wf, Tr) \qquad (5.3)$$

Our approach to obtaining a quantitative estimate of the size of the underground economy will be to model the demand for currency and to measure empirically the excess sensitive component of taxes and welfare benefits on currency.

Of course the methodology is subject to some limitations. We are assuming that only taxes and welfare benefits motivate participation when in fact there may be other factors that may be encouraging individuals and businesses to become involved in the cash economy. In Chapter Four we proposed a number of other factors affecting participation. Friends or family who consistently elude the authorities and public perception of government's use of tax revenue undoubtedly impact on whether an individual becomes involved or not. Unfortunately these variables are difficult to quantify. One could use proxies for these variables but the estimates are likely to be sensitive to the methodology used. Fortunately evidence suggests that the tax burden is by far the overwhelming factor affecting participation (Taylor, 2000) and consequently we expect the limitation to our approach to be quite minimal.

Estimation

To estimate equation (5.3) we use a number of data sources which can be found in Appendix 5D. In brief these are: real currency per capita (C) at constant 1989-90 prices; real disposable income (YD) at 1989-90 prices; interest rates paid on major trading bank fixed deposits (R); average income tax rate (T); welfare benefits as a percentage of disposable income (W); the rate of inflation (π); private consumption expenditure as a percentage of GDP and a dummy variable to account for the introduction of the GST (GSTD). The non-technical reader may skip the technical aspects of the model that follow and resume at the *Interpretation* section of this chapter without loss of continuity.

We first identify which variables in equation (5.3) follow a random walk. We begin by taking the logarithm of each variable and testing for a unit root. In levels all the variables exhibit evidence of a unit root but are clearly stationary when they are first differenced. The results are reported in Table 5.1.

Table 5.1 Dickey-Fuller Unit Root Tests

Variable Y_t		qd	Constant No Trend $\alpha(1)=0$ τ	Constant Trend $\alpha(1)=\alpha(2)=0$ F-test Φ_3
Log(C)	L	8	1.462	1.602
	D	8	-4.080	9.874
Log(YD)	L	11	1.342	1.053
	D	11	-2.974	5.456
Log(R)	L	11	-1.238	2.909
	D	4	-4.079	8.952
Log(π)	L	5	-1.447	2.422
	D	4	-4.774	11.800
Log(E)	L	10	-2.395	3.785
	D	10	-4.997	10.024
Log(T)	L	11	-2.435	2.989
	D	5	-3.796	7.597
Log(W)	L	5	-1.729	2.372
	D	11	-2.950	5.952

Notes: L denotes level series and D denotes first difference. (i) Columns 4 and 5 corresponding to L have the following Dickey-Fuller specifications:

$$\Delta Y_t = \alpha_0 + \alpha_1 Y_{t-1} + \sum_{i=1}^{q} b_i \Delta Y_{t-i} + \varepsilon_t$$

and Columns 4 and 5 corresponding to D have the following specifications (where t = time trend):

$$\Delta Y_t = \alpha_0 + \alpha_1 Y_{t-1} + \alpha_2 t + \sum_{i=1}^{d} b_i \Delta Y_{t-i} + \varepsilon_t$$

(ii) Null hypotheses are found at the head of each column. $\alpha(1)=0$ in columns 4 and 5 corresponding to L are τ-tests and in columns 4 and 5, $\alpha(1)=\alpha(2)=0$ are unit root tests with non-zero drift (F-test Φ_3). The critical τ-statistic for columns 4 and 5 corresponding to D is 2.57, and the critical F-test Φ_3 for columns 4 and 5 is 5.34.
(iii) d and q were chosen as the highest lag from the autocorrelation function of the first differenced series at the 95% confidence interval.

Since all the variables are I(1), regressing currency demand in first difference becomes an attractive option. The deficiency with such an approach is that we will be unable to account for long run behaviour in the demand for currency. Appropriately then we need a structure for currency demand that captures the short run adjustments, long run behaviour and also to be suitable for economic interpretation while at the same time satisfying the standard diagnostic tests; this suggests an error correction mechanism (ECM).

Our general specification for the ECM for currency demand takes the following form:

$$\Delta \ln(C_t) = \ln(\delta_0) + \delta_1 \Delta \ln(YD_t) + \delta_2 \Delta \ln(R_t) + \delta_3 \Delta \ln(E_t) + \delta_4 \Delta \ln(T_t)$$
$$+ \delta_5 \Delta \ln(W_t) + \delta_6 \Delta \ln(\pi_t) + \delta_7 D_2 + \delta_8 D_3 + \delta_9 D_4 + \psi_1 \ln(YD_{t-1})$$
$$+ \psi_2 \ln(R_{t-1}) + \psi_3 \ln(E_{t-1}) + \psi_4 \ln(T_{t-1}) + \psi_5 \ln(W_{t-1})$$
$$+ \psi_6 \ln(\pi_{t-1}) + \delta_{10} \ln(C_{t-1}) + \delta_{11} Tr + \delta_{12} GSTD + \mu_t \quad (5.4)$$

In equations (5.4) we introduce $\ln(C_{t-1})$ as an independent variable to capture the speed of adjustment $(1-\delta_{10})$ to fluctuations in currency demand by holders of currency and a deterministic seasonal component by a set of dummy variables as the original data series is seasonally unadjusted. We also introduce a dummy variable for the introduction of the GST (GSTD).[7] We tested for the possibility of endogeniety between currency, $\Delta \ln(C)$, and taxes, $\Delta \ln(T)$, disposable income, $\Delta \ln(YD)$, welfare benefits, $\Delta \ln(W)$, and consumption expenditure, $\Delta \ln(E)$, and found no evidence of endogeniety between these variables. We estimated an instrumental variable regression on each of the four independent variables and tested the significance of the predicted value when it is included in equation (5.4) (see Hausman, 1978). We report the results in the Table 5.2.

There are various alternative specifications that this currency demand model may have taken. In Tables 5.3 and 5.4 we report t-statistics on a MacKinnon, White and Davidson (1983) J-Test that tests the 'best fit' performances of these alternative specifications. The alternative specifications included a linear model, a double-log model, a log-linear model, a linear-log model and a seasonally adjusted error correction model.

In Table 5.3 we test an ECM, the null hypothesis, against various alternative model specifications. At the 1% level there is no evidence to reject the ECM for any alternative specification. We reverse the tests in Table 5.4. All the t-statistics are significant suggesting we can reject all the alternative specifications, the null hypotheses, when tested against the ECM. On the basis of these non-nested test an ECM turns out to be the most preferred equation and one we use for our estimation.

Table 5.2 Endogeniety Tests

Dependent Variable	Instruments $\sum_{i=1}^{N} \Delta \ln(Z_{t-i}), \sum_{i=1}^{N} \Delta \ln(C_{t-i})$		
$\Delta \ln(Z)$	t-statistics[a]		
	N=2	N=3	N=4
$\Delta \ln(T)$	1.219	1.627	0.441
$\Delta \ln(YD)$	-0.643	1.063	1.520
$\Delta \ln(W)$	0.275	-0.905	0.933
$\Delta \ln(E)$	-0.183	0.635	-0.758

Notes: (a) t statistic on $\Delta \ln(Z)$ when included as an independent variable in equation (5.4).

Table 5.3 MacKinnon-White-Davidson J-Test

	\multicolumn{5}{c}{H_1 (Alternative Hypothesis)}				
	Log-Log	Log-Lin	Lin-Log	Lin-Lin	SECM
Null Hypothesis H_0: ECM	0.5	0.1	1.0	2.1	0.1

Notes: (i) values represent t-statistics. (ii) The alternative specifications, all of which include the same variables, are defined as follows: **Log-Log:** a model linear in logarithms of the variables. Both the dependent and explanatory variables are in logarithmic form. **Log-Lin:** a semi-log model with the dependent variable expressed in logarithms and the explanatory variables are linear. **Lin-Log:** a semi-log model with only the explanatory variables represented in logarithmic form. **Lin-Lin:** Linear model. **SECM:** a seasonally adjusted ECM as defined in **Table 5.7** - *Measure of Robustness*.

Table 5.4 MacKinnon-White-Davidson J-Test

	H_0 (Null Hypothesis)				
	Log-Log	Log-Lin	Lin-Log	Lin-Lin	SECM
Alternative Hypothesis H_1: ECM	8.9	12.7	13.4	8.7	15.9

Notes: See Table 5.3.

In Table 5.5 we produce the results from estimating equation (5.4), using quarterly Australian data for the period June 1967 through to December 2000 in real per capita terms.

Most of the coefficients on the variables have the expected signs. The coefficient on interest rate is negative reflecting the opportunity cost on holding currency while the coefficient on disposable income is positive reflecting our expectations that for increases in economic growth there would arise a corresponding increase in the use of currency following increases in aggregate demand. The coefficient on the excess sensitivity of taxes is positive reflecting an incentive to conceal income from the tax authorities by demanding currency for the payments of goods and services. Interestingly the sign of the coefficient on welfare benefits is negative suggesting that those agents, who may be unemployed and receiving welfare benefits while working in the underground economy, trade-off work in the underground sector for more leisure when welfare benefits relative to their potential disposable income increases. The trend variable was found to be positive but insignificant and so it is not reported. It may be that such a variable is capturing both growing underground activities and technological development and producing a 'net' effect.

Table 5.5   Estimation Results

Dependent Variable: First Difference of (Natural) Logarithm of Real Currency per Capita (1967.2 to 2000.4)

Variable	Coefficient	t-ratio	Variable	Coefficient	t-ratio
Constant	0.071	0.17	$\Delta(\pi)$	-0.012	2.79
Ln(T)	0.057	2.11	Δln(W)	-0.031	2.11
ln(R)	-0.007	1.42	Δln(E)	0.138	3.00
Ln(π)	-0.010	3.23	Ln(C_{t-1})	-0.169	3.28
Ln(E)	-0.070	1.42	D2	-0.012	2.89
Ln(Y)	0.144	2.48	D3	-0.011	2.16
Δln(Y)	0.535	8.44	D4	-0.007	1.45
Δln(T)	0.157	4.69	GSTD	0.014	1.40
Δln(R)	-0.016	1.23			

Adjusted R^2 = 0.74   Durbin-Watson = 1.98
Number of observations = 135   RESET(3)$^{(a)}$ = 4.66
LM Statistic = 22.22   RESET(4)$^{(b)}$ = 3.08
ARCH = 1.76

Notes: (a) includes $\Delta\ln(C_t)^2$ as an additional regressor in eq.(5.4). (b) includes $\Delta\ln(C_t)^2$ and $\Delta\ln(C_t)^3$ as additional regressors in eq.(5.4).

Most of the *t*-statistics are significant at the 1% level and the adjusted R^2 is 0.74. The Ramsey (1969) RESET test shows no indication of mis-specification at the 1% level. Furthermore this specification for currency demand does not exhibit autocorrelated (Durbin and Watson, 1951) or heteroscedastic (ARCH) (Engle, 1982) disturbances. In Table 5.6 we report the calculated τ statistics for the Augmented Dickey-Fuller (ADF) equation with multiple lagged difference terms to test the existence of a unit root in the residuals.[8] Clearly the calculated τ statistics from the ADF equation are larger in absolute terms than the critical values. On the basis of such evidence we may infer that the regression equation is cointegrated.

Table 5.6 Properties of Residuals

No Constant, No Trend
$[\alpha(1) = 0]$

e(x)	e(0)	e(1)	e(2)	e(3)	e(4)	e(5)
τ	11.581	7.217	6.818	4.998	4.708	5.315

Notes: (i) e(x) where x indicates the number of lagged terms in the augmented Dickey-Fuller regression:

$$\Delta e_t = \alpha_1 e_{t-1} + \sum_{i=1}^{q} b_i \Delta e_{t-i} + \varepsilon_t$$

(ii) Null hypothesis is found at the head of the table: $\alpha(1)=0$. The critical τ-statistic is 5.028. See Phillips and Ouliaris (1990), p. 190.

Robustness

The results above, and their implication for the underground economy are robust across a variety of specifications. In the process of estimating different functional forms for currency demand an interesting result was observed, namely that the coefficients on the excess sensitivity variables were very similar. This implies that if we use these excess sensitivity components to estimate the size of the underground economy, our result will be relatively robust across different specifications of currency demand. In Table 5.7 we report the coefficients on the excess sensitivity variables from the ECM, equation (5.4), a double-log model and a seasonally adjusted ECM. These regressions produced similar parameters on the excess sensitive variables.

Table 5.7 Measure of Robustness – Excess Sensitivity in Taxes and Welfare Benefits

Equation No.	$\Delta \ln(T_t)$	$\Delta^k \Delta_s^F \ln(T_t)$	$\ln(T_t)$	$\Delta \ln(W_t)$	$\Delta^k \Delta_s^F \ln(W_t)$	$\ln(W_t)$
EQ 1	0.157	-	-	-0.03	-	-
EQ 2	-	0.14	-	-	0.01[a]	-
EQ 3	-	-	0.14	-	-	-0.03

Notes: (a) insignificant; (t-statistic = 0.29).
EQ1 is equation (5.4) while EQ2 is a seasonally adjusted error correction model specified as follows:

$$\Delta^k \Delta_s^F \ln(C_t) = \ln(\delta_0) + \delta_1 \Delta^k \Delta_s^F \ln(YD_t) + \delta_2 \Delta^k \Delta_s^F \ln(R) + \delta_3 \Delta^k \Delta_s^F \ln(E_t) + \delta_4 \Delta^k \Delta_s^F \ln(T_t)$$
$$+ \delta_5 \Delta^k \Delta_s^F \ln(W_t) + \delta_6 \Delta^k \Delta_s^F \ln(\pi_t) + \psi_1 \ln(YD_{t-4}) + \psi_2 \ln(R_{t-4}) + \psi_3 \ln(E_{t-4})$$
$$+ \psi_4 \ln(T_{t-4}) + \psi_5 \ln(W_{t-4}) + \psi_6 \ln(\pi_{t-4}) + \delta_7 \ln(C_{t-4}) + \delta_8 Tr + \delta_9 GSTD + \mu_t$$

where Δ_s denotes $1-L^s$ seasonal difference operator while F denotes the number of times this difference is applied. Δ^k denotes the level of differencing. In EQ2, F=1 and k=0. EQ3 is a Log-Log model:

$$\ln(C_t) = \ln(\delta_0) + \sum_{i=0}^{a} \delta_i \ln(YD_{t-i}) + \sum_{i=0}^{b} \psi_i \ln(R_{t-i}) + \sum_{i=0}^{c} \theta_i \ln(E_{t-i}) + \sum_{i=0}^{d} \upsilon_i \ln(T_{t-i})$$
$$+ \sum_{i=0}^{e} \lambda_i \ln(W_{t-i}) + \sum_{i=0}^{f} \beta_i \ln(\pi_{t-i}) + \sum_{i=1}^{g} \varphi_i \ln(C_{t-i}) + \alpha_1 D_2 + \alpha_2 D_3 + \alpha_3 D_4 + \alpha_4 Tr$$
$$+ \alpha_5 GSTD + u_t$$

Estimates of the Cash Economy

Using our preferred model, equation (5.4), and the estimation results from our regression in Table 5.5, we estimate the size of the underground economy in Australia as follows.[9] Rewrite equation (5.4) as:

$$\Delta \ln(C_t) = X\beta + T\alpha + W\delta + \varepsilon \qquad (5.5)$$

where
X = a 128×14 matrix of explanatory variables except the average tax rate and welfare benefits as a proportion of disposable income, namely

intercept, $\Delta\ln(YD)$, $\Delta\ln(E)$, $\Delta\ln(R)$, $\Delta\ln(\pi)$, $\ln(YD_{t-1})$, $\ln(E_{t-1})$, $\ln(\pi_{t-1})$, $\ln(R_{t-1})$, D2, D3, D4, GSTD, and $\ln(C_{t-1})$;

β = a 14 × 1 vector of coefficients corresponding to the explanatory variables in X;

T = a 128 × 2 matrix of two tax variables, namely $\Delta\ln(T)$ and $\ln(T_{t-1})$;

α = a 2 × 1 vector of coefficients corresponding to the tax variables in T;

W = a 128 × 1 vector of $\Delta\ln(W)$;

δ = the coefficient on $\Delta\ln(W)$;

ε = stochastic disturbance term.

The estimated currency for period t given observed average tax rates as well as welfare benefits is given by:[10]

$$C_t^* = \exp\left(X_t\beta + T_t\alpha + W_t\delta + \ln(C^*)_{t-1} + \Delta\ln(P)_t + \Delta\ln(N)_t\right) \quad (5.6)$$

where
P_t = GDP implicit price deflator;
N_t = population;
C^* = estimated nominal currency in the hand of the public in millions of dollars.

Now consider a situation in which we eliminate the excess sensitivity of taxes and welfare benefits that induce agents to participate in the underground economy. In other words, we assume that the currency demand function is no longer represented by an equation similar to (5.3) but rather an equation similar to (5.2a). Consequently in the absence of this excess sensitivity of taxes and welfare benefits, the volume of currency held by the public would be much lower. This is because there is no longer the need to demand cash for payment of goods and/or services in order to avoid detection from the authorities since there is no longer an incentive to work in the underground economy. This means that the currency level would settle at its 'natural' rate, a rate which we define as the stock of cash in the hands of the public in the absence of an underground economy. The estimate of this 'natural' level of currency (or legal currency) in period t when there exists no underground economy is given as:

$$C^*_{wt} = \exp\left(X_t\beta + \ln(C^*)_{t-1} + \Delta\ln(P)_t + \Delta\ln(N)_t\right) \quad (5.7)$$

Consequently illegal currency (defined as the sum of currency in the hands of agents engaging in underground activity) in period t is then defined as:

$$H_t = C^*_t - C^*_{wt} \quad (5.8)$$

$$= \exp\left(X_t\beta + \ln(C^*)_{t-1} + \Delta\ln(P)_t + \Delta\ln(N)_t\right) \times \left(\exp(T_t\alpha + W_t\delta) - 1\right) \quad (5.8a)$$

The velocity of circulation of currency in the legitimate economy in period t is thus:

$$V_t = Y^*_t \div C^*_{wt} \quad (5.9)$$

where
Y^* = GDP less consumption of fixed capital less net income paid overseas.[11]

If we assume that the velocity of currency in the underground economy is equal to that in the legitimate economy,[12] then multiplying the velocity of currency given by equation (5.9) to the volume of illegal currency, equation (5.8a), gives an estimate of the size of the underground economy. This is then expressed as a percentage of GDP. Figure 5.2 displays the size of the underground economy in Australia.[13] Yearly estimates are tabulated in Appendix 5C - Table 5C.1.[14] Appendix 5A details the methodology used to construct confidence intervals, which in contradistinction to a point estimate given here, takes into account the possibility that a sample estimate may differ from its true value because of sampling fluctuations. The narrow band width of the confidence intervals provided in the Appendix appears to reaffirm that the point estimates of the size of the cash economy in Australia are relatively robust. Interested readers may refer to this Appendix for further details. For the non-technical reader this may be skipped without loss of continuity.

Interpretation

There are three stylized facts of the cash economy evident from the evidence presented in Figure 5.1. First, the cash economy exhibits cyclical behaviour, which appears to coincide with the cyclical behaviour of the legitimate economy. Second, the cash economy in Australia has been relatively stable as a percentage of GDP, although there is some evidence of a mild decline at least during this period. This is not the case however for the period prior to 1978. Since 1978 the cash economy has averaged just shy of 15% of GDP. Third, in the lead up to the GST, the cash economy declined and the extent of this decline has by far exceeded any decline in the cash economy that has occurred during an economic downturn. This may be due to a number of factors including the impact of the tax mix and timing of consumption around the time of the introduction of the GST. To get a thorough understanding of cash economy in Australia we take a closer look at these three stylized facts.

Figure 5.1   The Cash Economy in Australia (% of GDP)

Stylized Fact One There is evidence in Figure 5.1 of at least four distinct cycles in the cash economy. The first cycle occurred between the late 1960s and early 1970s. During this period the cash economy reached a low of 13.4% of GDP and a high of 14.3% of GDP. The second cycle was longer in duration, averaging approximately six years, with a peak of about 15.7%

of GDP by 1974. The third cycle was shorter in duration lasting approximately five years and peaking in 1981 to about 15.5% of GDP. The fourth cycle occurred between 1984 and 1992 while the fifth cycle lasted approximately five years, peaking in 1996. A common feature of the underground business cycle is the similarity it shares with the ups and downs in the corresponding cycles of the legitimate economy. Later in this chapter we discuss at a greater length the relationship between the two cycles. The results suggest that there exists a procyclical behaviour between the economic cycles of the cash economy and the legitimate economy. In fact the findings suggest that not only are the cycles correlated (with a lag), but changes in economic conditions in the legitimate economy are found to drive similar changes in the cash economy.

The implications of this finding are quite serious. The findings suggest that legitimate business cycles are amplified by cycles in the cash economy. Consequently the greater the cyclical swings in the cash economy, the more unreliable are measures of business cycle data derived from national accounts. Policy makers attempting to smooth the business cycles are unaware of the true changes in economic fundamentals. It is quite possible that their policies are inefficient or ineffective in smoothing business cycle fluctuations.

Stylized Fact Two Although there is some evidence of a mild decline in the cash economy, the decline is not significant enough to warrant a change in the perception that subterranean activities in Australia have been anything other than entrenched in the way of life for many businesses and households. In fact during the period between 1978 and 1988 the cash economy on average measured about 14.8% of GDP, while from 1989 to December 1999, the cash economy measured on average 14.5% of GDP. The decline of 0.3% of GDP may be attributed to a faster growth rate in legitimate activities when compared to the growth in illicit activities. In fact the volume of illicit currency, calculated using equation (5.8a), has been growing over time which implies the size of the cash economy has been also been growing. It was however the anecdotal evidence through community perceptions that motivated the ATO in 1997 to establish the Cash Economy Task Force to deal with the growing non-compliance. These results only reinforce the earlier community perceptions.

Stylized Fact Three From 1998 until late-1999, the cash economy showed signs of moderate growth but from the end of March 2000 until September 2000 it experienced the sharpest decline reducing the cash economy to the lowest levels in decades. The cash economy had contracted by more than 1.5% of GDP to approximately 12.9% of GDP. By December

2000 activities in the cash economy crept upwards again reducing the fall of the previous quarter by 0.7% of GDP. The decline between March and September 2000 may be attributed to two factors – an *Expectations* and *Real Effect*. The rise in the cash economy in December 2000 may be due to the type of participants engaged in underground activities (*to be discussed below*) as well as business dissatisfaction with the GST transition process and the cash flow problems it has produced. It appears, based on this evidence, that the cash economy in Australia has shown strong signs of resilience to changes in the tax system. Unfortunately this is not good news for the government who has been expecting a windfall gain from falling participation in the cash economy.

Many of the sharp declines in the cash economy have been triggered by significant declines in legitimate economic activity. However the shortest and sharpest decline in the cash economy between March and September 2000 appear to have occurred in the absence of sharp decline in legitimate activity. The following *Expectations* and *Real Effects* may help explain this phenomenon.

Expectation Effect In the lead up to the introduction of the GST, the government advocated quite emotionally that the combination of the GST and the ABN would set in motion the processes that will ultimately eliminate the cash economy. It was true at the time that many consumers and businesses were unsure of how the GST would affect prices and market share. To those who traded in the cash economy the government was publicizing their fate. Potentially vulnerable at the prospect of being detected evading taxes, many participants may have reduced or halted trading in the cash economy until that time when they are confident with the operations of the new tax system. Therefore, given the significance of the tax reform, expectations may have played some part in reducing the size of the cash economy. How can we be sure? Typically the cash economy declines some time after a decline in legitimate activity. The significant decline in June 2000 seems to suggest that something other than a decline in opportunities has driven the fall. Since the decline occurred just before the introduction of the GST, our expectations hypothesis appears justified. There is no evidence to suggest that economic opportunities declined markedly between March and June 2000 to produce this result. In fact the GST and (to a much lesser extent) the Olympics had the effect of bringing forward expenditures to the first half of the year promoting economic growth. So it would be quite reasonable to suggest that the uncertainty with the new tax system drove a significant part of the decline in the cash economy for the quarter ending June 2000.

Real Effect The decline in the cash economy between March and September 2000 may not only be attributed to an expectations effect, but also a real effect driven by timing in consumption because of changes in the tax mix. In the lead up to the introduction of the new tax system many Australians brought forward much of their consumption to avoid the additional costs that the GST was expected to introduce. This contributed to the slow down in the second half of the year as consumption expenditure eased back. In fact GDP growth for the December quarter was reported at –0.6%, the first negative value since the recession in 1991. To help alleviate the down turn in the housing sector the Howard government re-introduced the First Homebuyer Scheme to subsidize first homebuyers in order to help stimulate aggregate demand. This appears to have had only but a moderate effect.

By overseas standards our estimates of the size of the underground economy in Australia is *relatively* high and this is clearly evident from Table 5.8. This perhaps may be alarming because although the underground economy in Australia has been relatively stable on average as a percentage of GDP, its size suggests that the underground economy is becoming more and more an accepted way of supplementing an existing income from the legitimate economy rather than the traditional second 'official' job. The previous estimate of the size of the underground economy in Australia, CBA (1980), is reported to be much lower than our estimate. The estimate in CBA (1980) is unreliable for two reasons: (i) the currency/demand deposit ratio approach, previously employed by Gutmann (1977), is highly sensitive to the base year chosen,[15] and (ii) other factors than the growth of the underground economy were driving the currency/demand deposit ratio, notably the reductions in demand deposits (Garcia and Pak, 1979). From Table 5C.1 (see Appendix 5C) we construct real tax collections for our entire sample period as an upper bound approximation to the potential revenue that the government is failing to collect as a consequence of under-reporting.[16] We construct this series by multiplying the size of the underground economy at any particular period to the average tax rate of the same period. Thus for 1997, in the absence of an underground economy, the government may have increased its revenue by an estimated $11.7 billion (at 1989-90 prices). For 1999 this would rise to $13.3 billion, an increase of approximately 13.6%.

Table 5.8   Comparative Estimates of the Underground Economy (% of GDP)

Country	Time Period	Size of Underground Economy	Study
Australia	1978-79	10.7%	CBA (1980)
	1970-00	14.7%	*this study*
New Zealand	1976	9%	Giles (1999b)
Canada	1976	3.5%	Giles (1999)
US	1976	11%	Gutmann (1977)
	1979	3.71-5.4%	Tanzi (1983)
UK	1977	2.3-3%	Dilnot and Morris (1981)
Sweden	1978	8-15%	Frey and Pommerehne (1984)
Germany	1974	4.8%	Petersen (1982)

Business Cycles

We address the issue of business cycles by proposing the following question. Does the existence of the cash economy and the variability of its cycle, have any implications for the nature of business cycles in Australia?

As we have already mentioned, our entire sample period is characterized by relative stability in the size of the underground economy on average as a percentage of GDP, yet over the same period the underground economy exhibited considerable fluctuations. These fluctuations may be positively or negatively correlated with the business cycle of the legitimate sector. What might we expect?

Suppose we observe a decline in legitimate economic activity. As incomes decline we would expect to see a decline in consumption of goods and/or services both in the legitimate and unofficial sectors. This is an 'income' effect. At the same time however, rising levels of unemployment generally follow the decline in legitimate activity as businesses lay off workers to compensate for falling demand. If these unemployed are enticed to work for any level of income offered in the underground sector, while receiving government assistance, we may in fact observe rising levels of subterranean activity, as these workers substitute into the cash economy. This is like a substitution effect. Which effect dominates will determine whether the cash economy moves pro-cyclically or counter-cyclically with the legitimate sector. If the income effect dominates we should observe a positive correlation between the growth rates of the two sectors and conversely if the substitution effect dominates.

In Figure 5.2 below we plot the real growth rates of the underground and legitimate sectors. We observe from Figure 5.2 that periods of downturn in our estimates of the underground economy coincide with downturns in the legitimate economy.

It turns out that the correlation between the real growth rates of the two sectors for the entire sample period is 0.48. In Table 5.9 we report the correlation between the real growth rates of the two sectors for the four distinctive cycles in Figure 5.2. The results suggest that for Australia the underground economy has been moving procyclically with the legitimate economy. Thus if consumers experience economic hardship over a particular period in the legitimate economy, the fall in consumption expenditure will dominate any offsetting effect of any activity emanating from the growing number of unemployed individuals accepting to participate in the underground economy. Consequently there is a direct spillover effect from the legitimate economy to the underground economy.

Figure 5.2   Real Growth Rates in the Legitimate and Underground Sectors (%) 1968-96

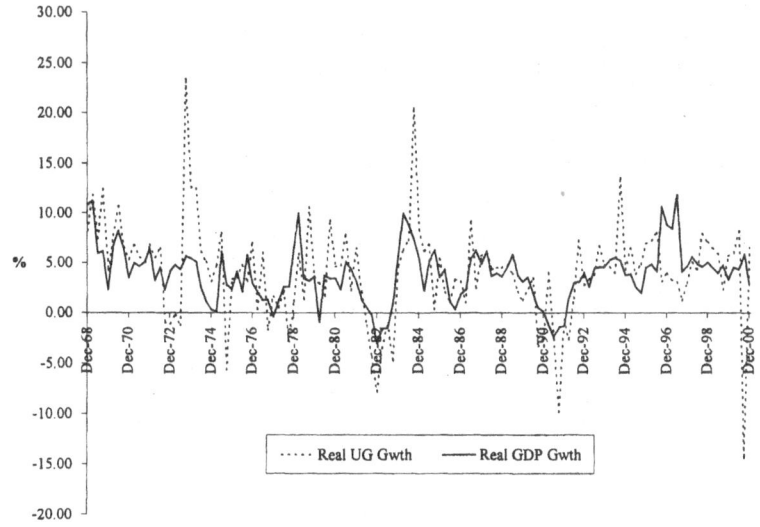

76   *Australia's Cash Economy*

The correlations in Table 5.9 do not address the direction of causation. We have to establish whether shocks in legitimate economic activity induce subsequent complementary shocks in the underground economy as well as whether the same shocks in the legitimate sector induce counter-cyclical disturbances in the underground sector via changes to the level of unemployment. Our inference from our discussion and from Figure 5.2, is that disturbances should originate from the legitimate economy and spill over to the underground economy, while changes in the level of unemployment, due to these same disturbances in the legitimate economy, should induce positively correlated disturbances in the underground sector. In Table 5.10 we report the results from applying Granger-causality tests. We report three, four and five lagged values of the two variables in each of the two regressions.

These tests reveal that the growth in the legitimate economy Granger-causes complementary procyclical changes in the growth of the underground economy. Similarly the growth in the number receiving unemployment benefits, due to the same growth in the legitimate economy, Granger-causes procyclical changes in the size of the underground economy. On the basis of these Granger-causality tests and the fact that the correlation between the growth rates of the two sectors is positive, we may infer that disturbances in the legitimate economy, which affect the level of income, dominate the effects of the same disturbance generated by rising levels of unemployment. Alternatively we may state that procyclical (counter-cyclical) fluctuations in the legitimate economy are tantamount to similar procyclical (counter-cyclical) disturbances in the underground economy. This suggests that business cycles that we observe from official statistics in Australia may under-represent the true extent of the business cycle in the aggregate.

To test the legitimacy of such a proposition we construct a total GDP series (TGDP) from the sum of the observable official GDP data and our estimated size of the underground economy. The growth rates of official GDP and TGDP series are reported in Table 5.11.

Table 5.9 Correlation and Covariance

	1968.2–2000.4	1968.2–1973.1	1973.2–1979.1	1979.2–1984.1	1984.2–1992.1	1992.2–1998.1	1998.2–2000.4
Corr	0.483	0.659	0.387	0.724	0.672	-0.189	-0.601
Co-Var	5.918	5.855	4.796	11.422	7.480	-1.027	-3.382

Notes: Corr denotes the correlation between the real growth rate of the official and underground sectors. Co-Var denotes the corresponding covariance between the real growth rates.

Table 5.10 Granger Causality Tests

	Null	A	F
EQ(1a)	U_G does not Granger cause Y_G	3	1.53
		4	0.92
		5	1.01
EQ(1b)	Y_G does not Granger-cause U_G	3	7.17
		4	5.78
		5	4.59
EQ(2a)	U_G does not Granger-cause L_G	3	0.31
		4	3.01
		5	2.59
EQ(2b)	L_G does not Granger-cause U_G	3	2.85
		4	4.72
		5	3.63

Notes: (i) The critical F statistics $F(\alpha, A, N-2A)$ are approximately: $F(0.01, 3, 101) = 3.95$; $F(0.01, 4, 99) = 3.48$ and $F(0.01, 5, 97) = 3.17$. The stnd dev of the dependent variables: $\text{Stdev}(U_G) = 2.41$; $\text{Stdev}(Y_G) = 13.02$; $\text{Stdev}(L_G) = 34.60$.

(ii) In the regressions Y denotes GDP as reported by ABS while U denotes our estimate of the underground economy. L denotes the number of individuals receiving unemployment benefits. The subscripts are defined as follows: G denotes that the variable is the nominal growth rate, and t denotes time t.

$$Y_{Gt} = \alpha_0 + \sum_{i=1}^{A} \alpha_{it} Y_{Gt-i} + \sum_{j=1}^{A} \beta_{jt} U_{Gt-j} + \mu_t \quad (1a)$$

$$U_{Gt} = \alpha_0^* + \sum_{i=1}^{A} \alpha_{it}^* U_{Gt-i} + \sum_{j=1}^{A} \beta_{jt}^* Y_{Gt-j} + v_t \quad (1b)$$

$$L_{Gt} = \delta_0 + \sum_{i=1}^{A} \delta_{it} L_{Gt-i} + \sum_{j=1}^{A} \rho_{jt} U_{Gt-j} + \varepsilon_t \quad (2a)$$

$$U_{Gt} = \delta_0^* + \sum_{i=1}^{A} \delta_{it}^* U_{Gt-i} + \sum_{j=1}^{A} \rho_{jt}^* L_{Gt-j} + \omega_t \quad (2b)$$

Table 5.11 Growth Rates of Real Income in Each Sector: Means and Variances

	1968.2-2000.4	1968.2-1973.1	1973.2-1979.1	1979.2-1984.1	1984.2-1992.1	1992.2-1998.1
U_G	[3.83]	[5.38]	[4.18]	[2.41]	[2.97]	[5.79]
	(21.93)	(15.17)	(29.21)	(24.29)	(21.67)	(5.49)
Y_G	[3.71]	[5.34]	[3.09]	[2.49]	[2.91]	[5.08]
	(6.84)	(5.19)	(5.49)	(10.26)	(5.72)	(5.34)
$TGDP_G$	[3.73]	[5.35]	[3.23]	[2.49]	[2.92]	[5.04]
	(6.90)	(5.50)	(5.78)	(10.79)	(6.38)	(3.91)

Notes: Subscript G denotes the real growth rate of the variable. U denotes the underground economy, Y denotes official GDP and TGDP is the sum of the two. Means in brackets and variances in parenthesis.

Clearly the variance of real official GDP (6.84) in Australia was lower than the variance of TGDP (6.90) for the entire sample period. With the exception of the periods 1968-72 and 1978-83 the variance of TGDP was larger than that of GDP for each of the last three business cycles. This implies that at least subsequent to 1983, Australia's true business cycle has been much more volatile that official statistics report. Consequently in the presence of a non-negligible and volatile underground economy, a nation like Australia may experience more volatility in its business cycles than would be inferred by the reported official statistics and this volatility would be more pronounced the larger and more volatile the underground economy becomes.

In Appendix 5B is a detailed business cycle analysis of the legitimate and underground economy in Australia. The result of this appendix reaffirms the conclusions that have just been drawn in the preceding paragraphs. There are a number of interesting results that may be drawn from the analysis of this appendix. We find that negative shocks in legitimate economic activity have a greater impact on the underground economy than do positive shocks. We also find that the underground economy appears to deepen the general business cycle but contributes less in comparison to its expansions. Interested readers may refer to this appendix for further details. For the non-technical readers this may be skipped without loss of continuity.

Summary

With increasing average tax rates and rising welfare benefits in recent years, many Australians have actively engaged in underground activities to supplement their disposable income. The amount of unreported income is at significantly high levels, averaging just shy of 15% of GDP or $64 billion (at 1989-90 prices) over the last ten years. This contrasts with estimates of the underground economy overseas that have on average been lower than for Australia, but large nevertheless.

Having estimated the size of the underground economy two interesting results came to light. First, shocks in the legitimate economy induced both an income and substitution effect via changes in income and unemployment and the former effect was found to dominate the latter. Secondly, and equally interesting, a significant and volatile underground economy was shown to have adverse implications on the nature of the business cycle in Australia, namely that the existence of a non-negligible underground economy generated more volatile business cycles.

It is imperative therefore that policy makers need to seriously consider the rules, regulations, taxes and welfare benefits that may have ignited enthusiasm for underground activity while launching initiatives to combat growing areas of non-compliance.[17] These approaches may need to be sector specific approaches rather than a singular broad reform that appears not to have worked successfully abroad. The next chapter helps shed some light on this issue as it identifies for the first time the likely contributors to the cash economy in Australia and the high-risk sectors that may need specific targeting.

Notes

1 See Garcia (1978), Feige (1979), Tanzi (1980), Tanzi (1983).
2 Carter (1984) provides no estimate of the underground economy in Australia while CBA (1980) provides only one (see Table 5.8).
3 We introduce the rate of inflation since the parameter restrictions in the Fisher Effect are unlikely to hold.
4 Although technology generally appears in lumps, given that there exists a lag between the time of discovery and implementation, the impact in reality will in fact be smooth so a time trend is a good approximation (Lieberman, 1979).
5 Because of the lack of appropriate data on marginal tax rates, (it is only available for males) we substitute this variable by an average tax rate. The marginal tax rate statistics that are available will exclude all activities of women and businesses that in our

definition would also form part of subterranean activities. Marginal tax rates are more appropriate however because an agent's decision to work in the underground economy is more likely to be affected at the margin. Although average tax rates may be a crude substitute, estimates by Zilberfarb (1986) using marginal tax rates for the United States produces very similar results to Tanzi's (1983) estimates based on the average tax rate. In our case we expect the use of average tax rates to produce similar results to what we would get if we had available the appropriate marginal tax rate statistics.

6   Such as Tanzi (1983), Klovland (1984), Isachsen and Strom (1985) and Zilberfarb (1986).

7   The seasonal dummied are defined as follows:

$$D_2 = \begin{cases} 1 & \text{for second quarter} \\ 0 & \text{otherwise} \end{cases} ; D_3 = \begin{cases} 1 & \text{for third quarter} \\ 0 & \text{otherwise} \end{cases} ; D_4 = \begin{cases} 1 & \text{for fourth quarter} \\ 0 & \text{otherwise} \end{cases}$$

GSTD is defined as 1 for the introduction of the GST (in this case on September and December 2000) and 0 otherwise.

8   Testing for a cointegrating relationship between the variables in the model are based on tests with no constant and no trend, since by construction the regression residuals have zero mean.

9   This approach is an improvement over Tanzi's (1983) method because it correctly uses the relevant excess sensitivity components in the currency demand function in order to quantify the size of the underground economy. Tanzi's functional form would underestimate the size of the underground economy.

10 Solving equation (5.4) for nominal currency holdings.

11 This measure is equivalent to National Income. We use this measure because both consumption of fixed capital and net income paid overseas are most likely to involve very small amounts of cash. In using these components we may be overstating the velocity of currency.

12 There is very little we can do about such an assumption.

13 In order to reduce the volatile short term fluctuations in the estimates, a 4 period centred moving average was constructed.

14 To simplify the presentation of the results, yearly estimates of the size of the underground economy as a percentage of GDP are provided.

15 Gutmann (1977) assumes no underground economy for the period 1937-41. Estimates of the underground economy are based on changes of the currency/demand deposit ratio of this period. The use of another base period would not only change the currency/demand-deposit ratio, but also the final results.

16 We make no inferences on these figures other than to get some idea about the possible magnitude of uncollected taxation revenue.

17 While this is a normative statement, constraining the growth in underground activities costs money. How much money is needed to reduce its size is a cost-benefit problem. This chapter has identified a pattern of behaviour and some costs (loss in tax revenue) but it is still necessary to weigh up the cost of enforcement etc.

Appendix 5A

Interval Estimation

Estimates of the underground economy can vary widely even within one country and have often given cause for concern about their reliability. For example in the United States, estimates of the 'true' extent of illicit behaviour have varied between 3% and 33% of GNP. Similarly for Sweden the estimates ranged between 7% and 17% of GNP, while for Germany between 8% and 24% of GNP (Frey and Pommerehne, 1984).

As opposed to the most standard econometric analysis, the underground economy literature gives only point estimates not standard errors. This makes it difficult to see if different estimates are contained within one confidence band. Part of the reason for this is that many of the methodologies used to estimate the size of the underground economy are not based in statistical or distribution theory. For example many are often based on voluntary surveys and samples (see Pestiau, 1983; Dilnot and Morris, 1981; and Censis, 1976), non-voluntary tax auditing (see Kinsey, 1987; Simon and Witte, 1982; and OECD, 1980), and labour market statistics (see Langfelt, 1989; Myrsten, 1989; and Frey and Pommerehne, 1984).

In Figure 5.1 of Chapter 5 we obtained point estimates of the cash economy in Australia for the period 1968 to 2000. However an interval estimate, in contradistinction with a point estimate, takes into account the possibility that a sample estimate may differ from its true value because of sampling fluctuations. Since each point estimate (given by 5A.1):

$$U\hat{G}_t = V_t \times \left[\frac{\exp(X_t\beta + \ln(C)_{t-1} + \Delta \ln(P)_t + \Delta \ln(N)_t) \times}{(\exp(T_t\alpha + W_t\delta) - 1)} \right] \quad (5A.1)$$

has variability around its mean and subject to sampling fluctuations, we cannot be certain that the unknown mean size of the underground economy is adequately represented by these point estimates. An assessment on the robustness of these estimates can be determined by constructing intervals for the underground economy at each data point. This appendix provides the first known approach to estimating confidence intervals for the estimates of the cash economy using a bootstrap methodology. We construct an interval from which we can be 95% confident that the unknown mean size of the underground economy lies between. However to do this we require the sampling distribution of (5A.1) and this is not known because of its unique calculation. It is possible however to approximate this distribution using a bootstrap procedure.

Method of Bootstrapping

The idea behind the bootstrap technique is as follows (see Veall, 1988; and Horowitz, 1997). Suppose a currency demand equation is given by:

$$\ln C = \Psi \rho + \varepsilon \qquad (5A.2)$$

where
Ψ is a $(n \times m)$ matrix of all the explanatory variables and intercept;
ρ is a $(m \times 1)$ vector of all coefficients; and
ε is an $(n \times 1)$ vector of white noise residuals.

The OLS estimated equation is given by:

$$\ln(\hat{C}) = \Psi \hat{\rho} + e \qquad (5A.3)$$

where
$\hat{\rho} = (\Psi'\Psi)^{-1}\Psi'\ln(C)$

The random error terms are assumed to have come from an unknown distribution with a mean of zero and a variance of σ^2. The result yields a vector of estimated residuals ($e_1, e_2, ..., e_n$). Suppose that $F(\varepsilon)$ takes any distribution. These values of the disturbance terms generate a vector of values for $\ln C(\ln C_1, \ln C_2, ..., \ln C_n)$ where:

$$\ln C_t = f(\Psi_t; \rho) + \varepsilon_t \qquad (5A.4)$$

Appendix 5A

The distribution will depend on the distribution function of $F(\varepsilon)$ but this unknown since we do not know the distribution of the ε terms. We are therefore prevented from getting a small sampling distribution for both $\hat{\rho}$ and $\ln(\hat{C})$. We can overcome this problem by using the bootstrap method because it allows the replacement of $F(\varepsilon)$ by $F(e)$. The estimated residuals then become:

$$e_t = \ln C_t - f(\Psi_t; \hat{\rho}) \tag{5A.5}$$

From this vector of estimated residuals a sample of size n is drawn with replacement, so that from this vector of estimated residuals, n residuals are randomly selected and a second vector of residuals is created. However each random selection is followed by replacement so that if e_1 is selected, it is replaced and has a probability of being selected again of $1/n$. In the extreme case, it is possible to have constructed a vector of estimated residuals from the original vector made up of a single estimate repeated n times, however the probability of this is very small. This second vector, e^* of re-sampled residuals, are substituted into equation (5A.2) and a new vector of estimated lnC^1 is generated holding of course the original estimate of ρ constant.

$$\ln C^1 = \Psi \hat{\rho} + e^* \tag{5A.6}$$

The vector Ψ remains unaltered throughout this procedure. Given the newly generated $\ln(C)$ we regress $\ln C^1 = \Psi \rho + \varepsilon$ in order to re-estimate ρ. The number of estimates of ρ will equal the number of replications that one performs. The process is repeated a large number of times and an empirical distribution of $\hat{\rho}$ is obtained which will serve as a proxy for the true distribution of $\hat{\rho}$. This distribution can be used to calculate a confidence interval for ρ.

A Modified Bootstrap

Because of the nature of our estimation we are concerned not with the empirical distribution of the estimated coefficients in the currency demand equation but rather the distribution of (5A.1).

Consequently a slight modification of the standard bootstrap routine was undertaken and the general process in estimating the confidence intervals for the underground economy in Australia for each data point may be summarized in the following seven steps.

1. Using the error correction model defined earlier to estimate the size of the underground economy, as:

$$\Delta \ln(C) = X\beta + T\alpha + W\delta + \varepsilon \tag{5A.7}$$

where ε_t is white noise, we estimate equation (5A.7) to obtain the estimates of $\hat{\beta}, \hat{\alpha}, \hat{\delta}$ and residuals $\hat{\varepsilon}_t$.

2. Sample randomly 119 white noise errors from 119 $\hat{\varepsilon}$ with replacement. Denote these re-sampled errors by $\hat{\hat{\varepsilon}}$.

3. Generate a new set of observations on the dependent variable by:

$$\Delta \ln\left(\hat{\hat{C}}_t\right) = X_t\hat{\beta} + T_t\hat{\alpha} + W_t\hat{\delta} + \hat{\hat{\varepsilon}}_t \tag{5A.8}$$

However since $\ln(C_{t-1})$ is an independent variable in the regression, for each new set of observations on the dependent variable in (5A.8), we solve for $\ln(C_t)$ (using $\ln(C_1)$ as the first observation) which we use in the next period as $\ln(C_{t-1})$. This dynamic bootstrap ensures consistent estimates of $\Delta \ln\left(\hat{\hat{C}}_t\right)$.

4. Regress $\Delta \ln\left(\hat{\hat{C}}_t\right)$ on X_t, T_t and W_t to obtain a new set of coefficients $\hat{\hat{\beta}}, \hat{\hat{\alpha}}, \hat{\hat{\delta}}$ and residuals $\hat{\hat{\varepsilon}}$.

5. Obtain the predictor of $\Delta \ln\left(\hat{\hat{C}}_t\right)$ based on these estimates as:

$$\Delta \ln\left(\tilde{C}_t\right) = X_t\hat{\hat{\beta}} + T_t\hat{\hat{\alpha}} + W_t\hat{\hat{\delta}} + \hat{\hat{\varepsilon}}_t \tag{5A.9}$$

6. Estimate the volume of illegal currency $\left(\tilde{H}_t\right)$ defined as the difference between the existing levels of currency holdings $\left(\tilde{C}_t\right)$ and a level estimated to be held when there exists no underground economy $\left(\tilde{C}_{wt}\right)$ - calculated as the holdings of currency in the absence of the excess sensitivity of taxes and welfare benefits.

$$\tilde{H}_t = \tilde{C}_t - \tilde{C}_{wt}$$
$$= \exp(\Omega_t) - \exp\left(\Omega_t - T_t\hat{\alpha} - W_t\hat{\delta}\right) \qquad (5A.10)$$

where $\Omega_t = ln(\tilde{C}_t) + ln(C_{t-1}) + \Delta\, ln(P_t) + \Delta\, ln(N_t)$

7. Finally estimate the size of the underground economy by:

$$U\tilde{G}_t = \tilde{H}_t \times \tilde{V}_t$$
$$= \tilde{V} \times \left[\begin{array}{l} \exp\left(X_t\hat{\beta} + ln(C)_{t-1} + \Delta ln(P)_t + \Delta ln(N)_t\right) \times \\ \left(\exp\left(T_t\hat{\alpha} + W_t\hat{\delta}\right) - 1\right) \end{array} \right] \qquad (5A.11)$$

We repeat steps (1) to (7), 10,000 times for each quarter in order to generate an empirical distribution of the predictor UG_t. By sorting out the 10,000 replications of UG in ascending order, we obtain 2.5 and 97.5 percentiles which we will use to construct the 95% confidence interval for our point estimates of the underground economy in Australia.

Bootstrap Results

In Table 5A.1 we report the lower (2.5 percentile) and upper (97.5 percentile) interval estimates constructed for the underground economy using the bootstrap procedure outlined in the previous section.

86 *Australia's Cash Economy*

The intervals are expressed both as a percentage of GDP (columns 4 and 6) and in millions of dollars, expressed in 1989/90 prices (columns 1 and 3). The point estimates are given in columns 2 and 5 of the same table. The empirical frequency distribution of the average bootstrapped estimates of the underground economy are given in Figure 5A.1.[1]

Table 5A.1   Interval Estimates of the Underground Economy[a]

Date	Lower Interval ($m)	Point Estimate ($m)	Upper Interval ($m)	Lower Interval (% of GDP)	Point Estimate (% of GDP)	Upper Estimate (% of GDP)
	(1)	(2)	(3)	(4)	(5)	(6)
1969	22276.39	25156.94	28125.65	12.22	13.80	15.43
1970	24114.03	27223.99	30429.78	12.48	14.09	15.74
1971	25560.43	28864.03	32271.80	12.57	14.19	15.87
1972	26005.88	29389.39	32870.20	12.37	13.98	15.63
1973	27977.38	31653.98	35433.13	12.62	14.29	15.99
1974	30859.13	34844.49	38934.04	13.66	15.42	17.23
1975	31027.90	35092.44	39261.80	13.38	15.13	16.92
1976	31877.79	36080.04	40409.42	13.25	15.00	16.80
1977	32505.05	36782.68	41176.44	13.38	15.14	16.94
1978	32190.16	36422.57	40770.64	12.85	14.54	16.27
1979	33799.80	38251.82	42828.98	12.83	14.52	16.26
1980	36187.65	40897.63	45747.40	13.41	15.16	16.95
1981	37776.13	42700.80	47775.89	13.51	15.27	17.09
1982	36883.10	41710.96	46692.04	13.26	15.00	16.79
1983	35252.34	39932.44	44746.32	12.56	14.23	15.94
1984	39431.49	44625.25	49980.05	13.02	14.73	16.50
1985	41488.10	46887.23	52455.06	13.16	14.87	16.64
1986	42617.89	48189.00	53936.86	13.27	15.00	16.79
1987	44519.03	50344.95	56341.75	13.24	14.97	16.76
1988	46191.43	52261.74	58502.35	13.18	14.91	16.69
1989	48405.48	54757.81	61292.78	13.25	14.99	16.77
1990	49056.11	55514.85	62156.67	13.24	14.98	16.77
1991	46735.30	52922.09	59284.69	12.82	14.52	16.26
1992	47316.39	53604.52	60080.36	12.60	14.28	16.00
1993	49520.33	56039.16	62755.74	12.68	14.35	16.07
1994	53364.68	60354.31	67563.61	13.03	14.73	16.49
1995	56330.03	63660.60	71231.75	13.33	15.06	16.86
1996	60217.00	68071.64	76180.40	13.32	15.06	16.85

Appendix 5A 87

Date	Lower Interval ($m)	Point Estimate ($m)	Upper Interval ($m)	Lower Interval (% of GDP)	Point Estimate (% of GDP)	Upper Estimate (% of GDP)
	(1)	(2)	(3)	(4)	(5)	(6)
1997	61033.81	69021.64	77262.42	12.61	14.26	15.96
1998	64329.44	72768.94	81485.39	12.66	14.32	16.03
1999	67498.88	76353.67	85492.81	12.77	14.44	16.17
2000.1[b]	16854.39	19063.96	21342.85	12.87	14.55	16.29
2000.2[b]	16734.84	18940.26	21211.06	12.30	13.92	15.59
2000.3[b]	15912.80	17997.36	20148.11	11.43	12.93	14.48
2000.4[b]	17441.56	19751.40	22135.87	12.02	13.61	15.25

Notes: (a) Based on December 31 each year.
(b) March, June, September and December quarters 2000 are quarterly estimates only.

Figure 5A.1   Empirical Frequency Distribution of Bootstrapped Estimates of the Underground Economy (% of GDP)

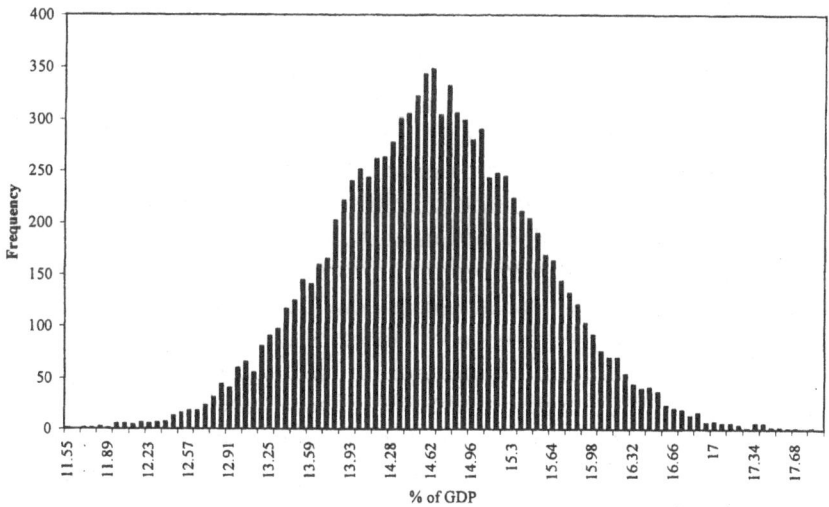

This distribution appears normal so it is acceptable to take the lower 2.5 percentile and upper 97.5 percentile to construct the intervals. In Figure 5A.2 we plot the interval estimates as a percentage of GDP for the entire sample period.

Figure 5A.2 Upper and Lower Bound Estimates of the Underground Economy (% of GDP)

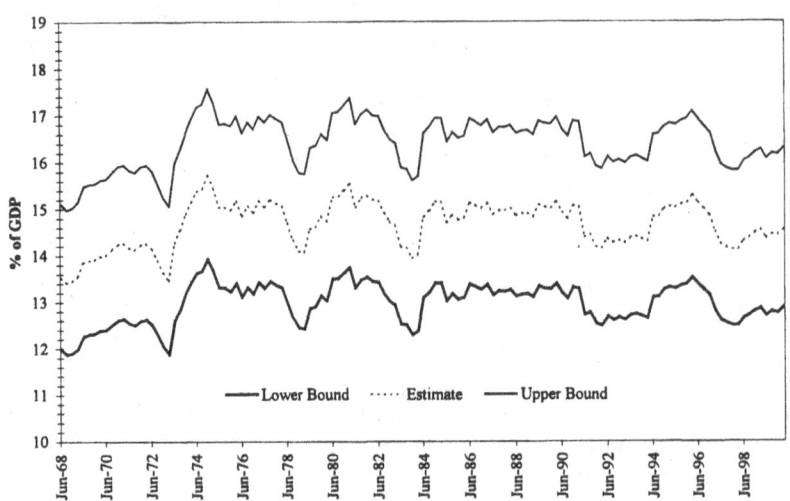

The bandwidth of the 95% confidence intervals is approximately 3% of GDP. The narrow bandwidth appears to reaffirms our earlier claim that the point estimates of the size of the underground economy in Australia are relatively robust. These confidence intervals can be interpreted as follows - we can say that we are 95% confident that the unknown mean size of the underground economy lies between the constructed intervals. For example, in 1969 we can say that we are 95% confident that the unknown population mean size of the underground economy to be between 12.2% and 15.4% of GDP. Equivalently the size of the underground economy is expected to measure between $22.3 billion and $28.1 billion. Similarly for 1995, we can say that we are 95% confident that the unknown population mean size of the underground economy lies between 13.33% and 16.86% of GDP. As recently as 2000, the interval is 12.2% to 15.4% of GDP or equivalently between $67 billion and $84 billion.

Prior to the publication of these results the cash economy was perceived to measure about 10% of GDP and assumed to be relatively constant over time.[2] However this estimate falls well outside the confidence bands and is unlikely to represent the true unknown mean size of the illicit activities in Australia. In fact it may be acceptable to denote the lower confidence interval as a lower bound estimate and the upper confidence interval as an upper bound estimate of the size of subterranean activities in Australia.

This confidence interval approach is directly applicable to existing methodologies used to estimate the size of the underground economy elsewhere and is likely to offer a better way to assess the reliability of point estimates. It is strongly recommended that interval estimates be used alongside existing point estimates to judge their reliability. It is quite possible that the various estimates of the underground economy in the United States are unreliable because their confidence intervals are very wide.

Notes

1   The single period distributions have very similar skewness and kurtosis as that represented by the average which is plotted in Figure 5A.1.
2   This is based on an earlier estimate of the size of the underground economy (CBA, 1980).

Appendix 5B

A Business Cycle Analysis of the Cash Economy in Australia

Over the last decade, hundreds of books and academic research papers have been written on the subject of business cycles. The seminal work of Burns and Mitchell (1947) some fifty years ago has provided a comprehensive reference guide to measuring and dating business cycles. Although their procedures involved much complexity and significant elements of self judgement (Baxter and King, 1995), procedures are now available to help identify business cycles without the complexity and this need for personal appraisal (Bry and Boschan, 1971). The procedures usually require the extraction of low frequency movements in the data before any identification of the phases of the business (growth) cycle is possible (see Van-Wel, 1998; Watson, 1994; Boehm and Liew, 1994; and Moreno, 1992).[1] The stylised facts of the business cycle are then investigated.

The aim of this appendix is to extend the standard business cycle analysis to the underground economy in Australia. We compare our results with those of New Zealand (Giles, 1997a, 1999a) and demonstrate that from these business cycle characteristics it may be possible to learn something about the behaviour of agents in the two sectors. It is also of considerable policy interest to know something about how the subterranean business cycle responds to legitimate economic activity. We find that the underground economy responds more to negative shocks in legitimate economic activity than it does to positive shocks. This implies that the underground economy may be deepening economic downturns and increasing the volatility of the business cycle in general.[2]

A typical business cycle can be described by identifying its period, amplitude and phase. We can define the period as simply the time between successive peaks or successive troughs. The amplitude of the cycle, on the other hand, is measured as the gap between a peak and its successive trough, or a trough and its successive peak. The phase of the cycle is defined as the movements from a peak to a trough (the contractionary phase) or from a trough to a peak (the expansionary phase). The best definition to date of the business cycle is that proposed by Burns and Mitchell (1947) which reads

> *Business cycles are a type of fluctuation found in aggregate economic activity of nations that organise their work mainly in business enterprise: a cycle consists of expansions occurring at about the same time in many economic activities, followed by similarly, general recessions, contractions, and revivals which merge into the expansion phase of the next cycle; this sequence of changes is recurrent but not periodic; in duration business cycles vary from more than one year to ten or twelve years; they are not divisible into shorter cycles of similar character with amplitudes approximating their own* (p. 3).

Burns and Mitchell (1947) in their definition were interested in the *Classical Cycle*, repetitive expansions and contractions in the absolute level of aggregate economic activity, that is, peaks and troughs in the level series.

Timing of Economic Fluctuations

The procedure implemented by the National Bureau of Economic Research (NBER) to determine the timing of peaks and troughs of the business cycle is a two stage procedure.[3] The first determines any local peaks and troughs for an individual series. There is a substantial amount of judgements involved in this first step but these are adequately replicated when using the Bry-Boschan (1971) program. The second stage involves identifying common turning points in each of the specific series analysed in Stage 1. If it is found that these specific cycles have corresponding and very persistent peaks and troughs, then the aggregate cycle, (or the *Reference Cycle*) is identified and its associated peaks and troughs are dated. Currently the NBER committee which oversees the dating of business cycles use data on income, aggregate output, trade and aggregate employment to identify timings of peaks and troughs (NBER, 1992), although there is a substantial publication lag to ensure that the published results are as accurate as possible (Stock and Watson, 1998).

Classical Cycles

There is a strong argument that favours business cycle research to be conducted using per capita data (see Diebold and Rudesbusch, 1989). The essence of this argument is that by doing so one can focus purely on the endogenous factors that generate the business cycle, omitting exogenous factors like population growth. In Tables 5B.1 and 5B.2 we report respectively the dates for the peaks and troughs of the classical legitimate and underground business cycle using real per capita measures.

Table 5B.1 Legitimate Classical Business Cycle Dates for Australia: Real Seasonally Adjusted GDP Per Capita

Real (1989/90) Seasonally Adjusted GDP Per Capita

Peak	Trough	Contraction P - T	Expansion T - P	Cycle P - P	Cycle T - T
8/60	8/61	12	-	-	-
2/74	8/74	6	150	162	156
8/76	11/77	15	24	30	39
5/81	2/83	21	42	57	63
8/85	5/86	9	30	51	39
2/90	5/91	15	45	54	60
Average Duration		13	58	71	71

What appears consistent between the dating chronologies of the underground and the legitimate economy is the asymmetry in the classical cycles. The average contractionary phase for both sectors is much smaller in duration than is the average expansionary phase, which suggests that both sectors are more responsive to economic downturns than they are to economic upswings. There appears also to be evidence from these results to confirm our earlier Granger-causality test we performed in Chapter Five. In that chapter we demonstrated that growth in the legitimate economy Granger-caused complementary procyclical changes in the growth of the underground economy. In Table 5B.3 we present results that show cyclical swings in the legitimate economy generate, with a lead, similar cyclical swings in the underground economy. This implies that the legitimate economy leads the underground economy or when the legitimate economy grows, subterranean activities grow also, but with a lag.[4]

Table 5B.2 Underground Classical Business Cycle Reference Dates: Real Seasonally Adjusted Domestic Product Per Capita

Real (s.a) Domestic Product of the Underground Economy (Per Capita)

Peak	Trough	Contraction P - T	Expansion T - P	Cycle P - P	Cycle T - T
5/72	11/72	6	-	-	-
8/74	8/78	48	21	27	69
11/81	8/83	21	39	87	60
8/89	8/91	24	72	93	96
Average Duration		25	44	69	75

Table 5B.3 Comparing Turning Points in the Legitimate and Underground Sectors Using Real Per Capita Measures (1966–96)

Legitimate Economy Classical Cycle		Underground Economy Classical Cycle		Lead (+) and Lags (-) (in months)	
P	T	P	T	P	T
2/74	8/74	8/74	8/78	6	48
8/76	11/77	ntp	ntp	-	-
5/81	2/83	11/81	8/83	6	6
8/85	5/86	ntp	ntp	-	-
2/90	5/91	8/89	8/91	-6	3

Notes: 'ntp' denotes no turning point.

Threshold Models

Models measuring asymmetric responses have been used recently to examine whether the asymmetric behaviour of the unemployment rate can be explained by movements in stock market return (see Silvapulle and Silvapulle, 1997; Domain and Louton, 1995; and Fama, 1981).[5] In this investigation we consider threshold models suggested by Tong (1990) and

Terasvirta (1990) to determine whether the subterranean business cycle responds to changes in economic conditions in the legitimate economy and exactly what the nature of these responses are. The question of how changes in legitimate economic activity affects the size and growth of the underground economy in Australia is quite important from a business cycle perspective. It is of considerable policy interest to know whether the cash economy softens a downturn in legitimate economic activity or deepens the downswing. If in fact the latter is true, a non-negligible underground economy will, in response to an economic downturn in legitimate economic activity, deepen the general business cycle. Policymakers who make use of official statistics to gauge their policies, may be unaware of the greater volatility of the business cycle generated by a sizeable underground economy. We have shown in Chapter Five that the underground economy does in fact increase the volatility of the business cycle in general. However in this appendix we are interested to know the extent by which the underground economy affects the business cycle - does it soften or deepen a downswing and does it contribute to enlarging an upswing?

This appears to be the first examination of its kind and it may serve policymakers well to know the results of this study. Although Giles (1999a) provided the first known empirical analysis for testing asymmetry for the growth cycle of the underground economy in New Zealand, the relationship between the underground and legitimate business cycles were not examined.

To undertake such an examination we begin with a simple autoregressive model reflecting the relationship between the legitimate and the underground economy. We use the result of Chapter Five that growth in the legitimate economy Granger-causes complementary procyclical changes in the growth of the underground economy. The model in its general form may be written as follows:

$$UG = \alpha_0 + \sum_{i=1}^{p} \alpha_i UG_{t-i} + \sum_{j=1}^{q} \phi_j GDP_{t-k} + \varepsilon_t \quad (5B.1)$$

for $t = 1,2,3,\ldots,N$

where UG and GDP are defined as the cyclical component of the underground and legitimate business cycle respectively after removing the stochastic trend using the Super Smoother (Friedman, 1984). In other words, each of the variables in (5B.1) are measured as deviations from the long term growth path.

By definition this model is a symmetric response model since the underground economy is affected symmetrically by positive and negative growth rates in legitimate economic activity. Lagged values of the regressand are introduced to capture any dynamic process, that is dependence of UG on its own past. Multiple lagged values of GDP are also modelled because legitimate business cycles were found to lead underground business cycles (see Table 5B.3). To test whether changes to legitimate economic activity have any effects on the cyclical fluctuations of the underground economy we test the hypothesis $H_o: \phi_i = 0$ against the alternative $H_1: \phi_i \neq 0$ for i=1,2,...q. In concordance with our results in Chapter Five we expect that legitimate activity will have a direct effect on activity in the underground economy. In fact we expect that the coefficient sum to be positive and significant.

There are two major limitations of equation (5B.1). First, it is a reduced form model which makes structural interpretations difficult because it is not possible to obtain estimates of the structural coefficients from the estimates of the reduced form coefficients. A structural interpretation is not an issue in what we do and so this limitation is not a constraint on the analysis that follows. Second, it is unable to identify whether positive (or negative) shocks in legitimate economic activity have predetermined effects on the cyclical variations of the underground economy around its trend growth path. That is, does the underground economy respond more to negative shocks in legitimate activity than it does for positive shocks? In order to measure these responses we modify equation (5B.1) as follows:

$$UG = \alpha_0 + \sum_{i=1}^{p} \alpha_i UG_{t-i} + \sum_{j=1}^{q} \left(\beta_j GDP_{t-j}^{+} + \delta_j GDP_{t-j}^{-} \right) + \varepsilon_t \quad (5B.2)$$

where
$$GDP_t^{+} = \begin{cases} GDP_t & \text{if } GDP \geq 0 \\ 0 & \text{if } GDP < 0 \end{cases} \quad \text{and}$$

$$GDP_t^{-} = \begin{cases} 0 & \text{if } GDP \geq 0 \\ GDP_t & \text{if } GDP < 0 \end{cases}$$

In equation (5B.2) the threshold level is set to zero along the trend growth path, that is, when economic activity rises above the trend, GDP is positive, denoted as GDP^+, and when it falls below, GDP is negative, denoted as GDP^-. By definition this model is capable of capturing responses to cyclical variations in subterranean output from negative and positive deviations in legitimate activity around its trend growth path. To test how the underground business cycle responds to changes in legitimate economic conditions we test the following two hypothesis: [1] To determine whether GDP^+ has any effects on economic activity in the underground economy we test null hypothesis H_o: $\beta_i = 0$ against the alternative H_1: $\beta_i \neq 0$; and [2] To determine whether GDP^- has any effects on economic activity in the underground economy we test the null hypothesis H_o: $\delta_i = 0$ against the alternative H_1: $\delta_i \neq 0$.[6] In all cases i=1,2,...,q.

We can also test using the same model (equation 5B.2) whether legitimate cyclical downturns (upswings) have steeper effects than do cyclical upswings (downturns) on the size of the underground business cycles. The appropriate hypothesis to test is H_o: $\delta_j = \beta_j$ against the alternative H_o: $\delta_j \neq \beta_j$. If we are interested in knowing whether negative shocks in legitimate activity have steeper effects that do positive shocks we substitute $\delta_j = \beta_j + \eta_j$ into equation (5B.2), which gives:

$$UG = \alpha_0 + \sum_{i=1}^{p} \alpha_i UG_{t-i} + \sum_{j=1}^{q} \left(\beta_j GDP^+_{t-j} + (\beta_j + \eta_j) GDP^-_{t-j} \right) + \varepsilon_t$$

(5B.3a)

$$= \alpha_0 + \sum_{i=1}^{p} \alpha_i UG_{t-i} + \sum_{j=1}^{q} \left(\beta_j (GDP^+_{t-j} + GDP^-_{t-j}) + \eta_j GDP^-_{t-j} \right) + \varepsilon_t$$

(5B.3b)

$$= \alpha_0 + \sum_{i=1}^{p} \alpha_i UG_{t-i} + \sum_{j=1}^{q} \left(\beta_j GDP_{t-j} + \eta_j GDP^-_{t-j} \right) + \varepsilon_t$$

(5B.3c)

Similarly to test whether positive shocks in legitimate activity have steeper effects than do negative shocks we substitute $\beta_j = \delta_j + \eta_j$ into equation (5B.2), which gives:

$$UG = \alpha_0 + \sum_{i=1}^{p} \alpha_i UG_{t-i} + \sum_{j=1}^{q} \left(\delta_j GDP_{t-j} + \eta_j GDP_{t-j}^+ \right) + \varepsilon_t \quad (5B.3d)$$

The new hypothesis, equivalent to H_o: $\delta_j = \beta_j$, may be stated as H_o: $\eta_j = 0$ against the alternative H_1: $\eta_j \neq 0$. Rejecting the null hypothesis in each case may imply that cyclical downturns (upswings) in legitimate activity generate relatively steeper cyclical downturns (upswings) in underground activity.

Results

The estimation process requires the identification of the appropriate values for the lag lengths, p and q. When choosing the appropriate lag length for bivariate models, two model selection criteria are most frequently used, the Akaike (1981) Information Cretiria (AIC) and Schwarz's (1978) Bayesian Information Criteria, (SBC). Equations (5B.1), (5B.2) and (5B.3c) are estimated using OLS with various lag lengths for p and q up to eight (8) lags, a total number of 64 combinations.[7] For lag lengths greater than six (6), the AIC values increase, therefore we consider models with lag lengths no greater than six (6). We choose, to ensure consistency of our results, the top five performing models for each of the equations (5B.1), (5B.2) and (5B.3c) according to the smallest AIC. In Tables 5B.4, 5B.5 and 5B.6 we report the top five lag length combinations for equation (5B.1), (5B.2) and (5B.3c) respectively.

Table 5B.4 Underground Business Cycle Responses to Cyclical Swings in the Legitimate Economy with a Symmetric Response Model

Lag Length	Coefficient Sum	F-Test
(2,2)	0.260	45.4
(2,3)	0.236	46.6
(3,2)	0.270	36.7
(5,5)	0.259	46.5
(3,3)	0.252	37.0

Notes: Both AIC and SBC information criteria identify that these lag lengths are the top 5 performing models.

In column 1 of Table 5B.4 are the preferred model specification. In column 2 we report the sum of the coefficients. Not only is the sum of the coefficients positive but every individual coefficient (not shown) is positive as well. This result is clearly consistent with our expectations that a procyclical relationship exists between the two sectors. In column 3, we report an F-statistic for the null hypothesis that the coefficients sum to zero. The calculated F-statistics are much greater than their critical values so we reject the null hypothesis that H_o: $\phi_i = 0$, that is, legitimate activity has a statistically significant effect on the activity in the underground economy. This conforms with our earlier results of Chapter Five.

The more important hypothesis test for determining whether GDP^+ and GDP^- have any effects on economic activity in the underground economy are reported in Table 5B.5. In Table 5B.5 it appears that negative shocks in legitimate activity impact more significantly on underground economic activity than do positive shocks. In column 1 of Table 5B.5 are the optimal lag lengths for equation (5B.2). In columns 2 and 3 of Table 5B.5 are the results for GDP^+. In column 2 we report a likelihood ratio (LR) test statistic (and p-value), a test that the coefficients on GDP^+ are jointly zero. Each of the LR test statistics are less than the critical χ^2 (5%) for all preferred models which suggests that we cannot reject the null hypothesis: Ho: $\beta_i = 0$. In column 3 we report the F-statistic (and p-value) for the null hypothesis that the coefficients sum to zero. With the exception of (1,1) all models fail to reject the null hypothesis that the coefficient sum for GDP^+ is zero. The results are somewhat different for the case of GDP^-. In column 4 we report the LR test that the coefficients on GDP^- are jointly zero. Based on the critical χ^2 (5%) we can reject the null hypothesis that H_o: $\delta_i = 0$. In column 5, we report the F-statistics for the null hypothesis that the coefficient on GDP^- sum to zero. In all models we reject the null hypothesis. These results suggest that negative shock in legitimate activity have a significant impact on underground economic activity but positive shocks do not. This has two implications: (i) expansions in legitimate economic activity have no predictive content for underground activity but contractions do; and (ii) contractions in underground economic activity resulting from contraction in legitimate economic activity may deepen the business cycle beyond that which is observed by policymakers from official statistics.

Table 5B.5 Underground Business Cycle Responses to Positive and Negative Shocks in Legitimate Economic Activity

Lag Length	GDP⁺ LR Test	GDP⁺ Coeff Sum	GDP⁻ LR Test	GDP⁻ Coeff Sum
(3,3)	3.02 [0.389]	1.1439 (0.962) [0.413]	13.92 [0.003]	2.290 (4.634) [0.004]
(4,3)	3.18 [0.365]	1.222 (1.010) [0.391]	12.55 [0.006]	2.149 (4.108) [0.008]
(4,4)	4.02 [0.403]	1.5138 (0.934) [0.447]	15.43 [0.004]	1.6594 (3.768) [0.007]
(1,1)	4.30 [0.038]	0.8388 (4.338) [0.040]	4.43 [0.035]	0.868 (4.482) [0.036]
(1,3)	4.27 [0.234]	2.4100 (1.384) [0.251]	10.51 [0.015]	0.726 (3.509) [0.018]

Notes: Figures in parenthesis are F statistics. *p*-values in brackets.

How does the magnitude of a contraction in legitimate economic activity compare to an expansion on underground activity? In Table 5B.6 we test the hypothesis that contractions in legitimate economic activity produce just as steep an effect as expansions on underground economic activity. The same table reports the top five lag length combinations for equation (5B.3c). For the top five lag length combinations, the calculated F-statistics falls well below the critical F value so we cannot reject the null hypothesis, H_o: $\eta_j = 0$. This implies that contractions in legitimate economic activity have as steep an effect as do expansions on the size of the underground business cycle.

Summary

We find a number of interesting results in this appendix that may be of some assistance to policymakers concerned with the size of the tax base and the underground economy. Not only do we find there to be a strong relationship between the business cycles of the legitimate and underground economy, but we also observe that the business cycle characteristics of the two sectors are very similar. Both sectors have classical business cycles that are asymmetric, with long expansions and violent contractions. Also, the legitimate economy was found to generate, with a lead, similar cyclical swings in underground economic activity. This activity however has contributed to increasing the volatility of the business cycle in Australia.

Table 5B.6 Testing Whether Negative Shocks have Steeper Effects than Positive Shocks on Underground Economic Activity

Lag Length	(3,3)	(4,3)	(4,4)	(1,1)	(1,3)
Coeff Sum (η_i)	1.147	0.927	0.694	0.029	0.735
F-Statistic	0.49	0.43	0.52	0.01	0.33
p-value	0.689	0.732	0.721	0.921	0.804

Using threshold models we arrive at a number of interesting results. First, changes in legitimate activity affect directly activity in the underground economy. This is consistent with the Granger-causality tests of Chapter Five. Second, negative shocks to legitimate economic activity appear to have a greater effect on underground economic activity than do positive shocks. That is, expansions in legitimate economic activity appear to have no significant predictive content for underground economic activity but contractions do. Third, contractions in legitimate activity do not produce significantly steeper underground business cycles than do expansions in legitimate activity. This suggests that not only does the underground economy fail to contribute significantly in enlarging a general economic upswing, but more importantly, it appears to be deepening the general economic cycle since contractions in legitimate activity were found to have a significant impact on underground activity while expansions did not.

Notes

1   This has been subject to much discussion primarily because different extraction processes may in fact affect business cycle dates.
2   We also demonstrated this conclusion in Chapter Five, but in a different manner.

Appendix 5B   101

3   This approach is very common in business cycle literature.
4   Our time period is not long enough to suggest definitely by how many months the legitimate economy leads the underground economy. Nevertheless it is fair to say that from this evidence, and that from Chapter Five, that the legitimate business cycle does lead the underground business cycle.
5   A similar study examines asymmetries in money supply shocks on output (see Cover, 1992).
6   A priori, I expect the coefficients to be positive for each of the two hypothesis because the business cycles of the legitimate and underground economy were found in Chapter Five to be procyclical. This in fact turns out to be true.
7   I find that testing the hypothesis in equations (5B.3c) and (5B.3d) produce the same result. Consequently I only report the results for equation (5B.3c).

Appendix 5C

Table 5C.1   Estimates of the Underground Economy in Australia (1967-96)

Year	Illegal Currency[a] ($m)	Legal Currency[a] ($m)	Underground Economy $m (1989/90 prices)	Underground Economy[b] (% of GDP)	Maximum Real Tax Collections ($m) (1989-90 prices)
1969	150.68	938.10	25156.94	13.80	3054.56
1970	169.63	1039.55	27223.99	14.09	3550.16
1971	190.50	1160.51	28864.03	14.19	3831.57
1972	208.17	1284.69	29389.39	13.98	3893.80
1973	248.08	1483.11	31653.98	14.29	4249.26
1974	308.89	1765.43	34844.49	15.42	5202.78
1975	368.30	2097.31	35092.44	15.13	5501.21
1976	429.98	2420.72	36080.04	15.00	5623.21
1977	487.82	2716.42	36782.68	15.14	5913.24
1978	535.64	3058.84	36422.57	14.54	5664.20
1979	603.19	3431.45	38251.82	14.52	5674.49
1980	689.18	3828.29	40897.63	15.16	6343.34
1981	786.97	4291.45	42700.80	15.27	6963.36
1982	864.48	4791.03	41710.96	15.00	6874.22
1983	935.22	5248.42	39932.44	14.23	6378.42
1984	1080.54	5967.92	44625.25	14.73	6977.26
1985	1244.29	6793.52	46887.23	14.87	7642.26
1986	1382.52	7412.68	48189.00	15.00	8179.88
1987	1531.61	8236.18	50344.95	14.97	8665.91
1988	1745.63	9350.84	52261.74	14.91	9041.55
1989	1925.70	10392.79	54757.81	14.99	9451.31
1990	2031.53	11085.54	55514.85	14.98	9643.92
1991	2223.04	12231.74	52922.09	14.52	9050.04
1992	2339.30	13074.04	53604.52	14.28	8616.53

Year	Illegal Currency[a] ($m)	Legal Currency[a] ($m)	Underground Economy $m (1989/90 prices)	Underground Economy[b] (% of GDP)	Maximum Real Tax Collections ($m) (1989-90 prices)
1993	2468.15	13822.07	56039.16	14.35	8768.63
1994	2653.52	14712.64	60354.31	14.73	9527.88
1995	2842.55	15421.44	63660.60	15.06	10625.90
1996	2990.91	16043.19	68071.64	15.06	11600.96
1997	3164.19	16897.48	69021.64	14.26	11702.26
1998	3390.10	18084.29	72768.94	14.32	12424.41
1999	3681.28	19441.38	76353.67	14.44	13312.66
2000.1	3831.84	19928.39	19063.96	14.55	3329.38
2000.2	3771.47	20721.74	18940.26	13.92	3310.72
2000.3	3236.17	21648.51	19723.13	14.17	3241.44
2000.4	4139.96	22074.79	20013.37	13.79	3182.46

Notes: (a) Based on December 31 each year.
(b) Average quarterly percentage of GDP over each year.

Appendix 5D: Data

Australian Data (Seasonally unadjusted values in millions of Australian dollars).

C   Currency, current prices. Source RBA Bulletin: Level of Monetary Aggregates - Table D.1.

T   Average Taxes, calculated as Direct Taxes on Incomes, current prices, (Source: ABS National Accounts: Income and Outlay Account - Commonwealth General Government - Table 5204-55) expressed as a percentage of GDP(I) (defined below).

W   Personal Benefit Payments, current prices. (Source: ABS Time Series Statistics: General Government Income and Outlay Account - Table 5206-33) expressed as percentage of YD (defined below).

YD   Disposable Income calculated as GDP(I) (income based and at current prices; Source: ABS Time Series Statistics: Domestic Production Account - Table 5206-23) less Direct Taxes on Incomes (as defined in T above) plus Personal Benefit Payments (as defined in W above).

E   Private Final Consumption Expenditure (current prices, Source: ABS Time Series Statistics: Household Income and Outlay Account - Table 5206-29) expressed as a percentage of GDP measured at current prices.

R   Interest Rates - Major Trading Bank Fixed Deposits. Source: ABS NIF-10s Model Database: Interest Rates and Exchange Rates - Table 1342-6.1.

L   Number of people receiving unemployment benefits. Source: ABS Time Series Statistics (Labour): Department of Social Security - Job Search and New Start Allowance Statistics - Table DSS-1.

π Implicit GDP [- expenditure based: GDP(E)] Price Deflator (see below).

The adjustment of Currency and Disposable Income into real per capita terms required the following series:

Appendix 5D 105

N   Population (000). Source ABS NIF-10s Model Database: Labour Market - Table 1342-21.

P   Price Deflator calculated as the ratio of GDP (expenditure based, current prices; Source: ABS Time Series Statistics: Domestic and Production Account - Table 5206-23) and GDP (expenditure based, 1989/90 prices; Source: ABS Time Series Statistics: Measures of GDP - Table 5206-1).

Y^* National Income: (used in calculating the velocity of currency). ABS Time Series Statistics: Table 5206-24: National Income and Outlay Account - Original.

6 Business and Household Participation

In this chapter we extend on the results of Chapter Five and provide the first decomposition of the cash economy into the contributions by households and businesses. The results will have an important implication for any government policy designed to target the cash economy. For example, if the household sector is found to be the largest contributor to the size of the cash economy, Australia's recent tax reforms are unlikely to have a significant effect on subterranean participation, as the new tax system isn't designed to deal with the household sector. In this instance separate policies may be required to stem growth in this sector. However if business participation dominates, these results may be used to assess the effectiveness of the new tax system on reducing business activity in the cash economy. Either way these results will be of assistance to those who are commissioned to deal with the underground economy.

In this chapter we undertake a number of initiatives. First we decompose Australia's cash economy into the contributions by households and businesses and examine their behaviour over time. Using these results we examine how changes in the tax incidence (the distribution of the burden of direct taxes on businesses and households) affects the volume of illicit behaviour. We follow this by a discussion on the possible sources of unreported activity and we make an attempt to rank a number of industry classifications according to their likely participation in the underground economy. The benefits of such an approach is that government may be made aware of the high risk sectors of the economy that may be actively participating in the cash economy. To set the scene however, we begin with a backgrounder into the recent changes to the tax system in Australia.

Tax Reform and the Cash Economy

The Federal government is expecting to make a substantial windfall gain from the introduction of the Goods and Services Tax (GST) which came into force on July 1, 2000. Government officials are expecting a tax net of $3.5 billion over the first three years, which spells some goods news for future Federal budgets. However much of this tax net depends on the success of the GST exposing these clandestine activities. The experiences abroad suggest the contrary. After the introduction of the GST in Canada in 1991 the size of the cash economy grew dramatically (Spiro, 1993), and similarly for the United Kingdom, which introduced a Value-Added Tax (VAT) in 1973 (Smith and Weid-Nebbeling, 1986). More recently, New Zealand introduced a GST in 1986, and immediately following its introduction the size of the cash economy fell substantially. However by 1994 the cash economy in New Zealand reached levels much larger than pre-1986, suggesting the GST has had little impact in reducing illicit activities (Giles, 1999).

The Effectiveness of the Australian Business Number

As part of the tax reform package, the government introduced an Australian Business Number (ABN) to make it easier for businesses to deal with government departments while improving the auditing process. The objective is to help identify false disclosure of income by businesses. Of course government officials are assuming that much of the cash economy is being generated by business participation. If on the contrary, consumers are participating to a greater extent in the cash economy, the ABN will prove ineffective in culling these illicit activities.

In principle the ABN should make it harder for businesses to operate in the cash economy. As part of the new Pay-As-You-Go (PAYG) system, any business-to-business transactions must quote an ABN on invoices. In the event that an ABN is not provided, the supplier of the good or service is required to withhold the top marginal rate of tax plus the Medicare levy (or 48.5%) from the business that receives the goods or services. If the business intends to claim an input tax credit on creditable purchases to offset the GST component, it must report an income received from the sale of those inputs. To help identify unreported income, the ATO has compiled a series of financial ratios for various industries as benchmarks to compare incomes and expenditures reported by individual businesses in their Business Activity Statements (BAS) – (see Table 6.1). The BAS is a single form used by businesses to report their tax entitlements (GST paid on inputs) and obligations (GST collected from the sale of goods and services) thereby reducing the costs of re-constructing the financial information provided by each individual business. This is expected to increase the efficiencies in the ATO's auditing processes.

Table 6.1 Benchmark Financial Ratios for Various Industries

Industry Classifications	Gross Profit (%)	Net Profit (%)	Wages Turnover (%)
Housing Construction	55-60	18-20	10-15
Fruit & Vegetable Growing	25-30	5-10	10-15
Clothing Manufacture	65-70	20-25	20-25
Restaurants & Cafes	60-65	10-15	20-30

Source: ATO (1998).

In Table 6.1 we present these financial ratios for a select number of industries. If either gross profit, net profit or wage to turnover ratios for a business are very different from the industry norm, it may warrant the ATO to investigate more closely the business concerned. Of course there a number of reasons why the difference may have occurred, but the use of these ratios allows a greater efficiency in identifying possible illicit activities taking place in the cash economy. Unfortunately the firm's books may be modified so the reporting may suit these financial ratios.

To accelerate ABN registrations, the government has made it explicit that any business, which continues to trade without any ABN, will be regarded as operating in the cash economy. However much of the ABN's success depends heavily on the nature of these clandestine activities. The cash economy typically has two types of transactions, namely business and household transactions, the latter the government concedes as the difficult component to expose. Business transactions include business-to-business and business-to-consumer transactions while household transactions make up the remaining consumer-to-consumer transactions. Which of these dominates the size of the cash economy will determine how successful tax reform and the ABN will be in curbing such activities. If household transactions make up the majority of the transactions taking place in the cash economy, it is unlikely that Australia's tax reform package will have any significant effect on eliminating illicit activities.

Business Transactions

The ATO has unveiled numerous attempts by businesses to conceal income earned in the cash economy in numerous business-to-business and business-to-consumer transactions. In most of these cases the offenders have been made to meet their tax obligations and fined in principle for the tax evasion. Some of the methods businesses have used to avoid detection in the past have been to explicitly request cash payment in return for significantly discounted prices for their services; keeping two sets of books - one for cash receipts and the other for non-cash receipts; failing to declare interest income; paying cash to employees in order to report lower levels of expenditures to justify the lower reported earnings; arranging for clients to purchase materials while the business provides the labour services; inflating expenditures; and invoice splitting, where labour and materials are recorded separately to circumvent the Prescribed Payments System.[1]

However with the introduction of the ABN, some businesses participating in the cash economy are at risk of being detected. If previously these businesses simply disclosed only some of their incomes and expenditures, the introduction of the ABN will make it much more difficult to continue this practice particularly for those concealing income from business-to-business transactions. For example, when Couriers Pty Ltd contracts with Mechanical Repairs Pty Ltd to service its fleet of vehicles both businesses are expected to disclose an ABN - Couriers to claim an input tax credit on the GST component of the contracted price and Mechanical Repairs to avoid Couriers withholding 48.5% and to ensure it can claim an input tax credit on the parts used to service the vehicles. So for most transactions, records of incomes and expenditures will be referenced by an ABN. Any attempt to mislead the ATO will be much more difficult, thereby discouraging inter-business misreporting of income and expenditure.

However some businesses may remain undetected if they deal directly with the consumer (business-to-consumer transactions) and are willing to forego the input tax credits on their expenditures, particularly if they believe that the returns from tax evasion are greater. The businesses in question may purchase inputs as 'consumers' absorbing the 10% GST, offer their services at subsidised prices, and concealing this income from the tax department. This is most likely to occur in occupations where the cost of labour services relative to the cost of physical inputs is very large. For example, computer service occupations are generally labour intensive and consequently much of total earnings is from labour service not from the sale of computer hardware (the physical inputs). In such circumstances the input tax credits, which the business is entitled to claim, would be much less than the tax savings if the business decided not to declare that income. However for occupations where the cost of labour services relative to the cost of physical inputs are small, participation in the cash economy may shrink. For example, forgoing an input tax credit from the sale of computer packages would far exceed the return from tax avoidance if the business decided to purchase computer packages as a 'consumer' and absorb the GST. Alternatively the consumer may purchase the inputs and the business provides the service for a price well below the legitimate market price. In this situation there is a Pareto Improvement to both the business and the consumer and such activities in the cash economy may continue.

Therefore the ABN is likely to have a significant impact on reducing clandestine activities arising from business transactions where the cost of labour services relative to the cost of physical input is small.[2] For those business transactions where the cost of labour services relative to the cost of physical inputs is large, the ABN is unlikely to have any significant impact on the size of clandestine activities, the tax-gap and therefore tax revenue.

Household Transactions

The ATO's track record in detecting illicit consumer-to-consumer transactions has not been as successful as for illicit business-to-business or business-to-consumer transactions. We use the term household transactions to identify individuals who are employees in the legitimate economy, but who outside of their official working hours, participate in the cash economy by offering the sale of goods and services to other consumers. For example, an employee of Mechanical Repairs Pty Ltd who accepts to repair a neighbour's car after work in return for payment is an example of a consumer-to-consumer transaction. Most often these payments are made in cash and never declared as income. Typically many of these consumer transactions are labour intensive, which suggests that the introduction of the ABN will never impact on these activities. As the customer is not entitled to claim an input tax credit on any purchase, an individual contemplating participating in the cash economy could easily profit by absorbing the GST on an input purchase and not disclose income received from the transaction. Alternatively the individual could ask the consumer to purchase the physical inputs and the labour services would be provided at a discounted rate. Only the value added from the labour services would constitute part of the cash economy.

The greater the volume of these household transactions to the overall number of transactions taking place in the cash economy, the less likely will tax reform impact on the size of the cash economy in Australia. In what follows below is an attempt to decompose the existing measure of the cash economy in Australia into business and household transactions. With this information we are in a better position to make some conclusive comments on the likely size of the cash economy following introduction of the GST in July 2000 and into the future.

Separating Business from Household Transactions

The approach taken to separate the contributions by businesses and households in the cash economy is a modification of the earlier approach taken in Chapter Five. In the section that follows we briefly outline the modifications that have been made. The non-technical reader may skip the technical aspects of the model that follows and resume at the *Interpretation* section of this chapter without loss of continuity.

In Chapter Five we specified the currency demand function as:

$$C = f(YD, R, \pi, E, Tr) \tag{6.1}$$

However for the purposes of identifying household and business contributions in the cash economy (6.1) could alternatively be written as:

$$C = f(Y - T_B - T_H + Wf, R, \pi, E, Tr) \tag{6.2}$$

where T_B and T_H is total direct taxation paid by business and persons respectively.

It is however the excess sensitivity of T_B, T_H and Wf on currency in which we are interested, that is, whether changes in taxes and welfare benefits changes currency holdings in addition to the effects of disposable income. Therefore we may estimate currency demand using the following new specification

$$C = f(Y - T_B - T_H + Wf, T_B, T_H, Wf, R, \pi, E, Tr) \tag{6.3}$$

Model

We begin by identifying whether the variables in question follow a random walk, namely we test for the presence of a unit root. The results are reported in Table 6A.1 in Appendix 6A. In levels all the data is $I(1)$ but is stationary when first differenced. Estimating our currency demand model in first difference is a possibility but doing so will fail to capture long-run behaviour in the data. An appropriate model which can capture both the short-run and long run characteristics and suitable for economic interpretation is an error correction mechanism. Using the MacKinnon, White and Davidson (1983) J-test we can show that an ECM specification of currency demand is preferable over a number of alternative specifications.[3]

The general specification for the ECM for currency demand is as follows:

$$\Delta \ln(C_t) = \ln(\delta_0) + \delta_1 \Delta \ln(YD_t) + \delta_2 \Delta \ln(R_t) + \delta_3 \Delta \ln(E_t) + \delta_4 \Delta \ln(T_{B,t})$$
$$+ \delta_5 \Delta \ln(T_{H,t}) + \delta_6 \Delta \ln(W_t) + \delta_7 \Delta \ln(\pi_t) + \delta_8 D_2 + \delta_9 D_3 + \delta_{10} D_4$$
$$+ \psi_1 \ln(YD_{t-1}) + \psi_2 \ln(R_{t-1}) + \psi_3 \ln(E_{t-1}) + \psi_4 \ln(T_{B,t-1}) + \psi_5 \ln(T_{H,t-1})$$
$$+ \psi_6 \ln(W_{t-1}) + \psi_7 \ln(\pi_{t-1}) + \delta_{11} \ln(C_{t-1}) + \delta_{12} Tr + \delta_{13} GSTD + \mu_t \quad (6.4)$$

We introduce three seasonal dummies as the data used in the modeling of currency demand is seasonally unadjusted. We also introduced a dummy to capture any possible structural change following the introduction of the GST (GSTD).[4] To capture the speed of adjustment to fluctuation in currency demand we introduce $\ln(C_{t-1})$ as an independent variable in the regression.

We also tested for the possibility of endogeneity between currency, $\Delta \ln(C)$, and income tax rates for wage and salary earners, $\Delta \ln(T_H)$, and resident businesses, $\Delta \ln(T_B)$, welfare benefits, $\Delta \ln(W)$, disposable income, $\Delta \ln(YD)$, and consumption expenditure, $\Delta \ln(CE)$, and found no evidence of endogeniety between these variables. We did this by estimating an instrumental variables equation on each of the five independent variables and tested for the significance of the predicted value when it is included in equation (6.4). The results for the instrumental variables regressions are reported in Table 6A.2 and the results from estimating equation (6.4) are reported in Table 6.2.

Many of the variables in Table 6.2 have the expected signs. The tax variable coefficients are significant at the 5% level and are positive as expected. This implies that an increase in the average tax rate is likely to motivate individuals to participate in the cash economy in an attempt to increase their disposable income. The coefficient on interest rates is negative as expected reflecting the increasing opportunity cost in holding currency balances when interest rates are rising. Surprisingly welfare benefit payments produces a negative coefficient. This suggests that increases in welfare benefits are not accompanied by a greater participation in the cash economy. On the contrary, the result suggest that whenever welfare benefits increase there is an incentive to trade off work in the cash economy for increase in leisure activities. The negative coefficient on the inflation variable is as expected, reflecting that rising rates on inflation erodes the value of money and encourages smaller volumes of currency holdings.

Table 6.2   Estimation Results

Dependent Variable: First Difference of (Natural) Logarithm of
Real Currency Per Capita (1968.2 to 2000.4)

Variable	Coefficient	t-ratio	Variable	Coefficient	t-ratio
Constant	0.0331	0.07	$\Delta \ln(T_B)$	0.1264	5.26
$\ln(T_B)_{-1}$	0.0267	2.29	$\Delta \ln(T_H)$	0.0727	2.42
$\ln(T_H)_{-1}$	0.0306	1.60	$\Delta \ln(R)$	-0.0210	1.62
$\ln(R)_{-1}$	-0.0082	1.51	$\Delta(\pi)$	-0.0113	2.66
$\ln(\pi)_{-1}$	-0.0102	3.56	$\Delta \ln(W)$	-0.0412	2.90
$\ln(E)_{-1}$	-0.0461	0.84	$\Delta \ln(E)$	0.1222	2.67
TR	0.0029	0.42	D2	-0.0103	2.52
$\ln(C_{t-1})$	-0.1554	3.19	D3	-0.0121	2.33
$\ln(Y)_{-1}$	0.1254	1.95	D4	0.0085	1.82
$\Delta \ln(Y)$	0.6168	9.81	GSTD	0.0260	1.89

Adjusted R^2 = 0.77
Number of observations = 134
LM Statistic = 22.22
ARCH = 2.169

Durbin-Watson = 1.83
RESET(3)[a] = 4.15
RESET(4)[b] = 2.75

Notes: (a) Includes $\Delta \ln(C_t)^2$ and $\Delta \ln(C_t)^3$ as an additional regressor in eq.(6.4).
(b) Includes $\Delta \ln(C_t)^2$, $\Delta \ln(C_t)^3$ and $\Delta \ln(C_t)^4$ as additional regressors in eq.(6.4).

Most of the t-statistics are significant at the 1% level and the adjusted R^2 is 0.77. The Ramsey (1969) RESET test shows no indication of misspecification at the 1% level. Furthermore this specification for currency demand does not exhibit autocorrelated (Durbin and Watson, 1951) or heteroscedastic (ARCH) (Engle, 1982) disturbances. In Table 6A.3 we report the calculated τ statistics for the Augmented Dickey-Fuller (ADF) equation with multiple lagged difference terms to test the existence of a unit root in the residuals. Clearly the calculated τ statistics from the ADF equation are larger in absolute terms than the critical values. This suggests the variables being co-integrated.

Separating the Contributions by Businesses and Households

Using our preferred model, equation (6.4), and the estimation results from our regression in Table 6.2, we re-estimate the size of the cash economy in Australia as follows. Rewrite equation (6.4) as:

$$\Delta \ln(C_t) = X\beta + T_H \alpha_1 + T_B \alpha_2 + W\delta + \varepsilon \qquad (6.5)$$

where
$X = $ a 128×14 matrix of explanatory variables except the average tax rate and welfare benefits as a proportion of disposable income, namely intercept, $\Delta\ln(YD)$, $\Delta\ln(E)$, $\Delta\ln(R)$, $\Delta\ln(\pi)$, $\ln(YD_{t-1})$, $\ln(E_{t-1})$, $\ln(\pi_{t-1})$, $\ln(R_{t-1})$, D2, D3, D4, GSTD, Tr, and $\ln(C_{t-1})$;
$\beta = $ a 14×1 vector of coefficients corresponding to the explanatory variables in X;
$T_H = $ a 128×2 matrix of 2 tax variables, namely $\Delta\ln(T_H)_t$ and $\ln(T_H)_{t-1}$;
$T_B = $ a 128×2 matrix of 2 tax variables, namely $\Delta\ln(T_B)_t$ and $\ln(T_B)_{t-1}$;
$\alpha_1 = $ a 2×1 vector of coefficients corresponding to the tax variables in T_H;
$\alpha_2 = $ a 2×1 vector of coefficients corresponding to the tax variables in T_B;
$W = $ a 128×1 vector of $\Delta\ln(W)$;
$\delta = $ the coefficient on $\Delta\ln(W)$;
$\varepsilon = $ stochastic disturbance term.

The estimated currency for period t given observed average tax rates as well as welfare benefits is given by:

$$C_t^* = \exp(X_t\beta + T_{H,t}\alpha_1 + T_{B,t}\alpha_2 + W_t\delta + A) \tag{6.6}$$

where
$A = \ln(C^*)_{t-1} + \Delta\ln(P)_t + \Delta\ln(N)_t$;
P_t = GDP implicit price deflator;
N_t = population and;
C^* = estimated nominal currency in the hand of the public in millions of dollars.

The extent of illicit currency in use is estimated by eliminating the excess sensitivity of taxes and welfare benefits from (6.6) such that:

$$C_{wt} = \exp(X_t\beta + A) \tag{6.7}$$

In the absence of these excess sensitive components we are in a position to construct measures of the volume of currency in circulation not driven by the intention to avoid paying income tax or welfare fraud. The stock of currency in the absence of these excess sensitive components is a measure of currency in the absence of a cash economy. However as we are more interested in determining the volume of illicit currency used by business and household transactions we consider two situations, one where we eliminate the excess sensitivity of taxes of resident businesses and the other, the excess sensitivity of taxes of wage and salary earners and welfare benefits. Therefore in the absence of these excess sensitive components we assume there is no demand for cash payment for goods and services in order to avoid detection. We can represent this natural level of currency holding for residential businesses as:

$$C_{wt}^B = \exp(X_t\beta_1 + T_{H,t}\alpha_t + W_t\delta + A) \tag{6.8a}$$

and for households as:

$$C_{wt}^H = \exp(X_t\beta_1 + T_{B,t}\alpha_t + A) \tag{6.8b}$$

Consequently illegal currency in period t used by resident business is:

$$H_t^B = C_t^* - C_{wt}^B$$
$$= \exp(X_t\beta + T_{H,t}\alpha_1 + W_t\delta + A) \times (\exp(T_{B,t}\alpha_2) - 1) \quad (6.9a)$$

while for wage and salary earners illegal currency is measured as:

$$H_t^H = C_t^* - C_{wt}^H$$
$$= \exp(X_t\beta + T_{B,t}\alpha_2 + A) \times (\exp(T_{H,t}\alpha_1 + W_t\delta) - 1) \quad (6.9b)$$

The velocity of circulation of currency in the official economy in period t is thus:

$$V_t = Y_t^* \div C_{wt} \quad (6.10)$$

where
Y^* = GDP less consumption of fixed capital less net income paid overseas.

Assuming that the velocity of currency in the cash economy is equal to that in the legitimate economy, we may multiply the velocity of currency in equation (6.10) to the volume of illegal currency given by equations (6.9a) and (6.9b).[5] This produces estimates of the size of illicit activities by resident businesses and wage and salary earners respectively. The sum of these estimates produces estimates of the size of the cash economy in Australia. In Figure 6.1 the contributions by resident businesses and the household sector to the overall size of the cash economy is presented.[6] To simplify the presentation of the results, yearly estimates of these figures are presented in Table 6B.1 of Appendix 6B.

Figure 6.1   Contributions by Business and Consumers to the Size of the Cash Economy in Australia (% of GDP)

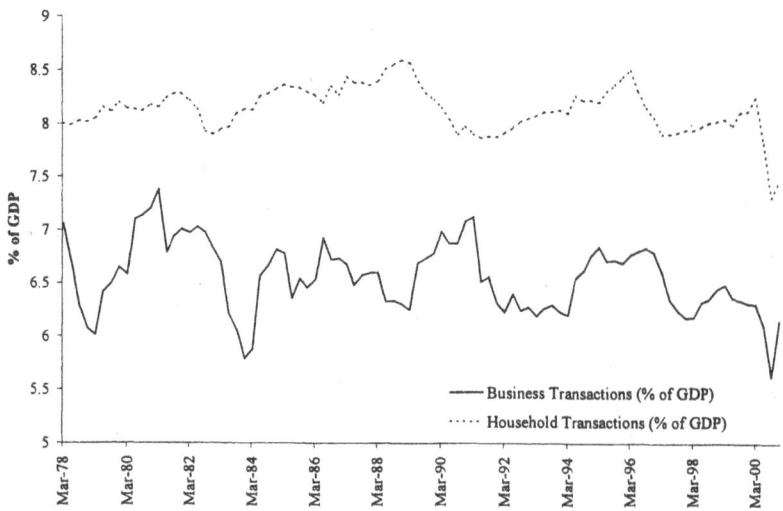

Interpretation

Figure 6.1 presents the results from the decomposition of the cash economy into the contributions by businesses and households. For the first time we have information on the types of contributions. Up until now the government has presumed that much of the activities taking place in the cash economy was due to business participation. In fact the government was enthusiastic about the implementation of the ABN as a way of curbing back much of this business participation because the ABN monitored business activities. However Figure 6.1 suggests the contrary - that much of the activities taking place in the cash economy in Australia are the result of household transactions not business transactions.

This result has a serious implication for the effectiveness of the ABN. Since the ABN specifically targets businesses, it is unlikely to have any effect on household contributions. On average the household sector contributes about 55% of the illicit transactions taking place, while the other 45% is attributed to businesses. This suggests that more than half of the cash economy will certainly continue to thrive under the new tax system unless a new strategy is taken to tackle household contribution. Of the 45% of business transactions that may be identified in the cash economy, many may not necessarily surface as legitimate transactions. In fact it may be the case that once detected these activities cease altogether. Clearly the government is restricted in raising the maximum 45% of the tax gap in Table 6B.1 of Appendix 6B. Similar policies, which target the household sector, may reduce illicit household activities, but may not generate the expected revenue if these activities fail to surface because they cease to exist.

What is also very notable in Figure 6.1 is the relatively sharp decline in the cash economy in the lead up to the introduction of the GST. From Figure 5.2 the cash economy declined by more than 1.6% of GDP. Over half of the decline is attributed to a contraction in household transactions (0.94% of GDP) and the remainder is due to falls in business transactions (0.68% of GDP). Although the decline appears more pronounced for the household sector, the business sector contraction was of the same magnitude (11%) from March to September 2000. However this decline is not solely attributed to the introduction of the GST. In the December 2000, the national accounts recorded a negative growth in GDP that coincided with the general decline in the leading economies worldwide. The combined effect of the GST and the economic slowdown contributed to one of the largest declines in the cash economy since the mid-1970s. Typically any economic slowdown in legitimate activity brings with it a slow down in subterranean activities. However in the two quarters leading up to the introduction of the GST the legitimate economy was growing and the cash economy declined. The most plausible explanation for this is the propaganda that preceded the GST. With public perception that the GST was targeted to eliminate the cash economy, many businesses and households feared detection. Much of the fear may have been driven by a lack of understanding of how the new tax system works. Unlike any other contraction, this contraction in the cash economy was not induced by a decline in economic activity, but rather an announced change in government policy. The problem with this expectation effect is that once the workings of the tax system are better understood this decline may reverse into an upswing. This may have occurred to some limited extent in the December quarter in which the size of the cash economy was estimated to have grown by 0.7% of GDP from the previous quarter.

International evidence of the cash economy in countries, that have introduced similar reforms to their tax system, have experienced similar phenomena, although they appear not to have been so dramatic. Over time however much of this decline reversed and the size of the cash economies grew once more, in some cases at levels above those before the introduction of tax reform. With public perception that the GST was targeted to capture much of the cash economy by exposing all forms of illicit activities, many businesses and consumers feared exposure and anecdotal evidence seems to suggest that much of the activities were scaled down or even ceased temporarily.

What is very notable in Figure 6.1 is the volatility of the two series. Household transactions appear relatively stable with downturns in underground economic activities coinciding (but not perfectly) with the major downturns in the legitimate economy. Business transactions are much more volatile than are consumer transactions, although the major downturns coincide more closely with major downturns in legitimate economic activity. Consequently much of the volatility that is observed in Figure 5.1 is the result of the volatility in business contributions of Figure 6.1. These results appears to mirror the results in the national accounts that suggests that much of the volatility in the measure of economic growth stems from the volatility of legitimate investment expenditure. From Figure 5.1 many of the sharp downswing in underground economic activity have come from downswings in illicit economic contributions by businesses. For example, in 1982-3 the decline in the cash economy by 1.5% of GDP (or 10% of its size) was predominantly attributed to the decline in business transactions. In fact over this period there was a steady growth in household transactions in the cash economy. A similar result is evident for the decline of illicit economic activities during 1991-92. The fall in the size of the cash economy by an average of 1% of GDP (or 7% of its size) was predominantly due to falls in business transactions. Household transactions during this time increased by 0.11% of GDP. These offsetting changes to business and household transactions during the course of the business cycle ensured that the size of the cash economy in Australia remained largely stable at average of 15% of GDP. It appears that the GST in Australia has had little effect on reducing activities in the cash economy.

Simulating the Relationship between the Cash Economy and the Tax Incidence

The cash economy serves as the vehicle by which many economic agents escape the inspections and regulations of government. We have already discussed many of the implications that may arise from a significantly large

120   *Australia's Cash Economy*

and volatile cash economy. In this section we will be concerned with how changes in the tax incidence (the distribution of the burden of direct taxes between wage and salary earners and businesses) affects the volume of illicit behaviour. The tax incidence that we consider will include changes in the tax burden of businesses and consumers. In particular we will look closely at the following three questions:

i) How changing the total tax burden affects participation in the cash economy?
ii) How changing separately the tax burden of businesses and consumers affect participation in the cash economy? and,
iii) How changing welfare benefits affects consumer participation in the cash economy?

In light of a growing cash economy any government must unwilling embrace a fall in taxation revenue as a consequence of a shrinking tax base. Daunted with spending decisions and commitments, the government, in response to a fall in tax revenue, may attempt to supplement this shortfall by either raising taxes, maintaining current expenditure by running larger budget deficit or simply cutting back on government spending (Houston, 1987). However raising taxes to compensate for the shrinking tax base may drive more individuals into the cash economy or encourage existing cash economy participants to work more extensively. Consequently this may further shrink the tax base and tax revenue may continue to fall. The effects may be further compounded as higher taxes discourage investment and savings.

The size of the tax gap, or the amount of tax owed but not voluntarily paid, has been rising steadily in real terms since the early 1960s (see Table 5C.1 of Appendix 5C). In Figure 6.2 we plot the size of the federal budget deficit adjusted for the possibility that (i) one-quarter of the cash economy is detected and taxed and (ii) that three-quarters is detected the taxed. For example, if it were remotely possible to have detected three-quarters of all illicit economic activity and successfully tax it, the federal budget deficits, particularly during 1972, 1974, 1980-82, 1990 and 1995-96 would have been reported as surpluses instead. If on the other hand, the government had only been able to expose and tax one-quarter of the entire cash economy, the federal budget would have moved from deficit to surplus only during 1982.[7]

Figure 6.2 The Federal Budget Deficit: Reducing the Tax Gap

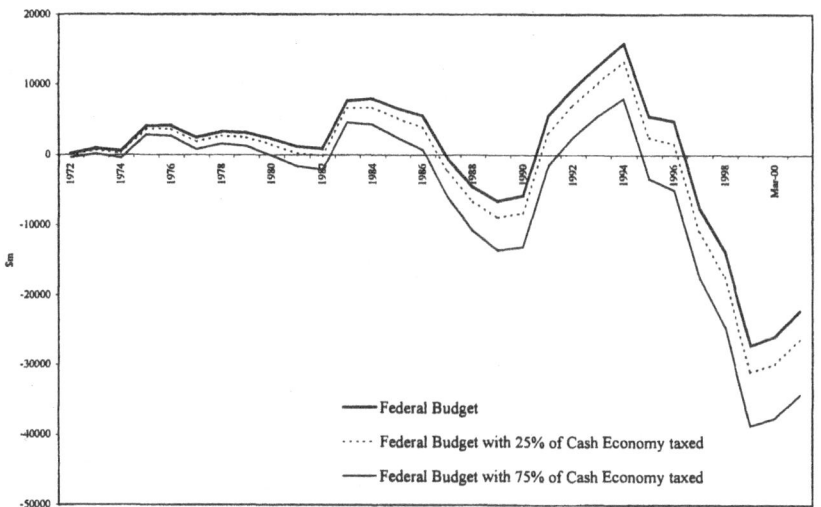

Undoubtedly the most appropriate means by which to reduce the tax gap is to implement policy initiatives that monitor and discourage participation in the cash economy. In Australia the introduction of the GST and the ABN are in some respects attempts by the government to reign in these illicit activities. Below we examine how sensitive the cash economy is to changes in a number of macroeconomic policy initiatives, under the old and in the new tax environment. In particular we will be interested in comparing the effects of four fiscal policy measures on the cash economy.

Policy One Total tax burden is reduced by 10% for both businesses and households while welfare benefit payments remain unaltered.
Policy Two Welfare benefit payments are set to 5.1% of disposable income - the average for the late 1960s when the cash economy was reported to be much smaller.
Policy Three Total tax burden is reduced by 10% for households only.
Policy Four Total tax burden is reduced by 10% for businesses only.

Although we consider reductions in both the level of taxes and welfare benefits, we should not expect the results to be symmetric to those arising from equal increases in taxes and welfare benefits. For given penalties and probabilities of detection, any increases in taxes would most likely increase the cash economy by more than a similar tax cut. *Why?* Individuals may be more reluctant to participate in the cash economy for the first time, but once they cross over, it may not follow that symmetrical reductions will bring them back (see Houston, 1987). Consequently we should regard the impact of these four policies on the size of the cash economy as lower bound estimates. The results for each of these four policies are given in Table 6.3. In column 3 of Table 6.3 we report the effects on the size of the cash economy pre-GST and in column 4 of the same table, the effects on the size of the cash economy post-GST.

We discuss briefly the results from the simulation of the four policy proposals below:

Policy One To investigate the effects of a cut in average tax rates on the size of the cash economy we assume, ceteris paribus, the total tax burden is reduced by 10% equally for both businesses and consumers. We assume that the values of α, β and δ remain constant. The new estimate of the cash economy as a percentage of GDP is given in Table 6.3. It appears that by reducing the total tax burden by 10%, the size of the cash economy contracts in size by 4% (or 0.58% of GDP) before the introduction of the GST, and by 4.2% (or 0.6% of GDP) post GST. Taking note of business and consumer transactions separately, we find that reducing the total tax burden by 10%, reduces, on average, illicit consumer transactions by 3.9% and business transactions by 4.1% (pre-GST), while post-GST the effects were 4.2% and 4.3% respectively. The results suggest that tax cuts affect illicit consumer transactions more than business transactions post-GST. This implies that Fiscal Policy affecting consumer disposable income is likely to change the size of the cash economy to a greater extent than from affecting business profitability and it appears to be more sensitive since the implementation of the new tax reform package. Although similar conclusions are drawn from the remaining three policy proposals, it may be too early to make any definite conclusions on this because we lack a full comprehensive set of data post-GST.

Policy Two This alternative policy targets welfare benefits to be 5.1% of household disposable income, a rate which prevailed during the late 1960s and when the cash economy appeared to be much smaller that for subsequent years. Since March 1990 welfare benefit payments as a percentage of disposable income have measured 10.8%. The results are presented in Table 6.3 and suggest that reducing welfare benefit payments to 5.1% of household disposable income increases the size of the cash economy by 0.2% in the period before the introduction of the GST and by 0.3% after the introduction of the GST. This may mean that those who are receiving welfare benefits and participating in the cash economy would increase their participation in these illicit activities whenever there is a fall in welfare benefit payments. This effect appears more pronounced after the introduction of the GST. This may be consistent with expectations that the average increase in the cost of goods and services will promote greater participation amongst those on welfare benefits up until some point where they trade work for leisure. As evident in Table 6.3, changing welfare benefits affects the cash economy to a lesser extent when compared to changes in the tax rate.

Table 6.3 Effects on the Cash Economy from Changes to Average Taxes and Welfare Benefits

		Pre-GST Average % change in the size of the Cash Economy	Post-GST Average % change in the size of the Cash Economy
Policy One	Business	-4.1	-4.3
	Consumer	-3.9	-4.2
	Total	-4.0	-4.2
Policy Two	Business	0.0	0.0
	Consumer	0.3	0.4
	Total	0.2	0.3
Policy Three	Business	-0.2	-0.2
	Consumer	-3.8	-4.0
	Total	-2.1	-2.3
Policy Four	Business	-3.9	-4.2
	Consumer	-0.1	-0.2
	Total	-1.9	-2.0

Notes: The average size of the cash economy as presented in Figure 6.1 is (i) for business transactions (6.7% of GDP); (ii) for consumer transactions (7.9% of GDP); and (iii) for aggregate transactions (14.6% of GDP).

Policies Three and Four Policy Three simply extends on Policy One, examining the impact of reducing the total tax burden for households by 10%. Policy Four repeats the exercise, but the focus is on the tax burden of business, which for comparison's sake, is also reduced by 10%. The results from Policy Three suggest that a 10% fall in the average tax rate reduces the size of the cash economy by 2.1% (or 0.3% of GDP). Much of the fall is driven by consumer transactions, which fell by 3.8% pre-GST and 4.0% post GST. Policy Four suggests that when reducing the tax burden for businesses by 10% the size of the cash economy declines by 1.9% (or 0.2% of GDP) and that much of the decline is driven by business transactions which fall 3.9% pre-GST and 4.2% post-GST. In both Policies Three and Four, the effects, post-GST, appear to dominate the effects pre-GST. Possibly this may be due to the fact that since the introduction of the GST much of the distribution of tax collections has changed. There is now a greater proportion of total tax revenue collected from indirect taxes than was the case prior to the change in tax policy.

Using these four hypothetical policy measures, we showed that changes in taxes dominate changes in welfare benefits in affecting the size of the cash economy. This we suggested to be because taxes were evidently the major factor encouraging participating in the cash economy. Generous welfare benefit payments appear to encourage more leisurely activity rather than encourage additional work in the cash economy. This implies that there are very few who have chosen the combination of income from welfare benefits and illicit income as a strategy for accumulating a larger disposable income. In fact, it may be the case that those who are unemployed and in receipt of welfare benefits participate in the cash economy simply to maintain a preferred standard of living and would reduce the amount of work in the cash economy if welfare benefits were to increase. This appears to be the finding in Table 6.2.

We find some very interesting results from these simulation exercise, namely that (a) changing the tax burden and the tax incidence affects the cash economy more significantly after the introduction of the GST; (b) reducing the total tax burden by 1% reduces the size of the cash economy by 0.05% of GDP pre-GST and by 0.06% of GDP post-GST; (c) reducing the tax burden of consumers by 1% reduces the size of the cash economy by 0.032% of GDP pre-GST and by 0.035% post-GST while reducing the tax burden for businesses by 1% reduces the size of the cash economy by 0.025% of GDP pre-GST and by 0.03% of GDP post-GST; and (d) targeting welfare benefits to 5.1% of disposable income as was the case during the late-1960s, the size of the cash economy would rise by 0.03% of GDP pre-GST and by 0.05% of GDP post-GST.

Sources of Unreported Activity

In possession of a decomposition of the cash economy into the contributions by households and businesses, it is possible to forge a relationship between the types of industry and their participation in the cash economy. Decisions by government to target select industries that it regards to be actively engaged in the cash economy, is more often based on perception rather than evidence. The consequences are significant if the perceptions are wrong. If, for example, the government targets the primary production sector of the economy because it perceives it to be the largest contributor to the cash economy, when in fact it contributes very little, implies a significant misuse of financial resources. Knowing which industries are more prone to actively participate in the cash economy helps for an efficient allocation of resources being used to combat the cash economy and increases the likelihood of raising tax revenue.

To avoid misappropriating financial resources in this way, we provide the first known ranking of a select group of industries according to their participation in the cash economy. To determine this ranking we require knowledge on the motives that encourage participation. Although we have identified a number of these factors in Chapter Four, we have argued that changes in tax burden are a major factor driving participation. Of course, changes in regulation and income tax reporting requirements may cause much anxiety in the business community and this may motivate participation in the cash economy. But such variables are difficult to quantify accurately. Being in a position to account for all the factors affecting different industry participation in illicit activities would produce a robust ranking of this participation. However we lack such quality data and we use the tax burden to proxy many of these other variables that may affect a business's willingness to meet its tax obligations.

To produce such a ranking, we construct a tax rate elasticity that captures the responsiveness of changes in the size of the cash economy to a change in the tax burden for business. Consequently such a ranking is based on the likelihood of participation in the cash economy from changes in the tax burden rather than simply from a dollar measure of the industry's contribution to the cash economy. This approach has several advantages. First, it highlights industries that are active in the cash economy and identifies the type of evasion occurring. Second, it highlights the industries likely to engage in more active participation if there are adverse changes to economic conditions. Obtaining a dollar measure of the size of each industry's contribution to the cash economy will not provide the necessary information to identify those industries that are more prone to changes in economic conditions. Therefore the use of elasticities contributes significantly in identifying the industries that are more susceptible to become involved in illicit activities.

Previously much of the arbitrary ranking used by government officials to target particular industries was based on the opportunities available to entrepreneurs to avoid income tax. For example, the housing construction industry has been the subject of close examination by the ATO because many opportunities were seen to exist for tradesmen to evade income tax. Not surprisingly we find that the housing construction industry is very sensitive to changes in economic conditions and appears to be one of the leading industries contributing to the size of the cash economy.

We consider a number of industries, both small and large, which may be prone to participate in the cash economy. In column 1 of Table 6.4 we report the major industry categories, including the various industry sub-categories (in column 2). The data was obtained from various annual Taxation Statistics publications published by the Australian Taxation Office. Data spans the period 1982 to 1999 and covers wage and salary earners, small and large businesses. Small businesses are defined as sole traders and partnerships and large businesses are defined as the remaining cohort of companies and other businesses. All of the conclusions drawn from these results apply only to the pre-GST period.

Table 6.4   Businesses by Industry: Broad and Fine

Broad Industry	Fine Industry
Primary Production	**Horticulture and fruit growing** (e.g. vegetable growing, fruit growing, etc)
	Marine fishing (e.g. prawn fishing, and other forms of marine fishing)
	Poultry farming (e.g. eggs, etc)
Manufacturing	**Clothing, footwear and leather products** (e.g. men's and women's wear manufacturing, etc)
	Wood, wood products and furniture (e.g. kitchen, office and home furniture, etc)
	Metal products (e.g. sheet metal furniture manufacturing, etc)

Broad Industry	Fine Industry
Construction	**House construction** (e.g. concreting services, bricklaying services, roofing services, plumbing services, electrical services, painting and decorating services, landscaping services, etc)
Retail trade	**Food** (e.g. takeaway food retailing, bread and cake retailing, fresh fish retailing, etc)
	Other personal and household goods retailing (e.g. furniture retailing, pawnbroking, antiques retailing, flower retailing, etc)
	Motor vehicle services (e.g. smash repairing, automotive electrical services, motor vehicle brake and clutch repair and service, etc)
Accommodation, Cafes & Restaurants	**Hotels, motels, boarding houses, etc.** (e.g. accommodation, etc)
Transport	**Transport** (e.g. long and short distance bus transport, taxi service, parking services, travel agency services, road freight services, etc)
Services	**Services** (e.g. surveying services, data processing services, computer maintenance and consultancy services, legal services, accounting services, secretarial services, pest control services, cleaning services, hairdressing and beauty salons, child minding services, etc)

We have since found that a major determinant affecting the size of the cash economy to be the tax burden on businesses and consumers. In the first part of this chapter we obtained a precise measure of this effect when we decomposed it into the effects on businesses and households. In this section we take this a step further and construct elasticity coefficients that measure the responses to changes in the tax burden for consumers and selected industries on the size of the cash economy. The average tax rate elasticity for illicit transactions for business in industry i is calculated as $\partial \ln(H^B \times V) / \partial \ln(T_{I,i})$ and for consumers as $\partial \ln(H^H \times V) / \partial \ln(T_w)$, where $T_{I,i}$ denotes the average tax rate for industry i, and T_w, the average tax rate for wage and salary earners. The results are presented in Table 6.5. We can use these elasticity coefficients to measure the likelihood of participation in the cash economy. The larger the elasticity the greater the likelihood of participation. These elasticity values may then be used to rank industries by participation for a given tax burden.

128   *Australia's Cash Economy*

In Table 6.5 are three elasticity measures - column 2 for consumers, column 3 for small business and column 4 for large business. As expected the elasticity measure for consumers is much larger than for either small or large businesses. This result is consistent with the findings reported in Figure 6.1 that consumer transactions dominate the volume of transactions taking place in the cash economy. The elasticity measure implies that a 1% change in the average tax rate increases the size of the cash economy by 0.217% of GDP. What is more interesting from the results of Table 6.5 is that small firms participate much more actively in the cash economy than do large businesses. This is true for all industry classifications given in the table.

These results provide the opportunity to rank particular industries by the participation in the cash economy. The ranking for both large and small businesses in each of the industry classifications are denoted in square brackets. Considering small business first, the services sector appears to be the biggest contributor to the cash economy in Australia. This is no great surprise because big opportunities exist for substantial income tax savings in an industry where much of the input into production are labour services. In Table 6.4 is a selected list of fine classifications for the services sector. Much of these services are typically paid in cash and it is difficult to keep an adequate monitor on the volume of such transactions taking place. For example, a small hairdressing business can report a given number of haircuts per day to the ATO and the remainder form tax free earnings which will almost certainly be difficult to detect. Much, if not all, of these transactions are settled in cash and no physical records exist should the tax office require an audit.

Table 6.5   Ranking Business and Consumer Contributions to the Cash Economy in Australia

Industry Classification	Consumers Tax Rate Elasticity (η)	Small Business Tax Rate Elasticity (η)	Large Business Tax Rate Elasticity (η)
Wage and Salary	0.217	-	-
Services	-	0.167 [1]	0.018 [5]
Construction	-	0.133 [2]	0.024 [2]
Retail	-	0.106 [3]	0.025 [1]
Primary Production	-	0.089 [4]	0.009 [7]
Manufacturing	-	0.088 [5]	0.021 [4]

Industry Classification	Consumers Tax Rate Elasticity (η)	Small Business Tax Rate Elasticity (η)	Large Business Tax Rate Elasticity (η)
Restaurants, Cafes & Accommodation	-	0.071 [6]	0.013 [6]
Transport	-	0.025 [7]	0.025 [2]

Notes: Ranking of industry according contributions to the cash economy are given in square brackets.

Ranking second in its contribution to the cash economy is the construction (housing) industry. The tax rate elasticity of 0.133 for the construction industry implies that for every 1% increase in the average tax rate, the size of the cash economy increases by 0.133% of GDP. The ATO's earlier attempts to monitor the activities in the construction industry are warranted by this result. It is known that if, for example, you require the services of a bricklayer, plumber or even concreter, it is always possible to negotiate a much cheaper price if the payment is made in cash. For this reason it became 'industry practice' to undertake some additional work in the cash economy.

Ranking third in our set of broad classifications for small business is retail trade. Examples of retail trade susceptible to illicit activities may include: the takeaway corner stores, smash repairs, mechanical and electric repair of motor vehicles, flower retailing etc. The results suggest that increases in the average tax rate by 1% increases the contribution by the retail sector to the size of the cash economy by 0.106% of GDP.

Next in our ranking is primary production, followed by manufacturing, restaurants, and cafes and the transport services sector. Although the taxi industry is measured in the transport services sector, an increase in the average tax rate increases the size of the cash economy by a marginal 0.025% of GDP. This suggests that even if the taxi industry was neck deep in illicit activity, the volume of undeclared income from the taxi industry could not be compared to the volume of illicit activities taking place in the construction industry, for example. In the months leading up to the GST, taxi drivers were frequently the subject of discussion on tax evasion and portrayed as a key factor in the cash economy. These results suggest this to be far from the truth. The construction industry alone was failing to report at least five times more income than was being undisclosed to the tax office by the transport industry (including taxi drivers).

In column 4 of Table 6.5 are the results of the average tax rate elasticity for large businesses. The results suggest that the ranking of industries by their contribution to the cash economy is much different for large businesses. In fact taking the first position in the list of most dominating factors are retail trade followed closely by construction and transport. Last in the ranking is primary production, which given the nature of the activity should not be surprising. Most of the activity in the primary production industry for large business generally involves thousands of hectares of plantations compared to the small scaled operations. The smaller scaled farming operations have the opportunity to sell small volumes of agricultural products to local market distributors for cash to avoid being detected evading tax. For this reason the ATO implemented a Reportable Payments System to circumvent these activities from taking place. Agricultural businesses who invest in large volumes of agricultural products would find it much more difficult to evade taxes in ways that may be available to the smaller farmer. From the results of Table 6.5, the cash economy in Australia has been largely driven by small business, with large businesses contributing a smaller component of transactions in the cash economy.

Next we construct an average tax rate elasticity measure for all groups by regional areas. We have taken the regions to be the States of Australia. With such information it becomes feasible to target not only a specific industry but the state in which those industry are more prone to participating in the cash economy. The results of these findings are presented in Table 6.6.

Table 6.6 Ranking State's Contributions to the Cash Economy in Australia

	NSW	VIC	QLD	SA	WA	TAS
Tax Rate Elasticity (η)	0.17 [1]	0.07 [4]	0.07 [4]	0.01 [5]	0.09 [2]	0.08 [3]

Notes: Ranking of states according to contributions to the cash economy are given in square brackets.

The evidence appears to suggest that much of the cash economy in Australia is taking place in the state of NSW. The elasticity measure implies that for every 1% increase in the average tax rate in NSW, the cash economy increases by 0.17% of GDP. The remaining states appear to contribute much less. Western Australia, although ranks second to NSW, contributes much less and compares very closely to Tasmania's contribution, which ranks third, and Victoria and Queensland, which rank equal fourth. South Australia appears to contribute the least to the size of the cash economy. The results of Tables 6.5 and 6.6 together imply that small businesses in NSW rank ahead of small business in other states when it comes to participation in the cash economy.

Notes

1. With the introduction of the GST, the Prescribed Payments System and the Reportable Payments System will be abolished and replaced by the Pay-As-You-Go (PAYG).
2. Needless to say, this does not suggest that all illicit business activities will be eliminated.
3. We undertook similar non-nested tests to test an ECM, the null hypothesis, against the various alternative model specifications, namely log-linear, log-log, linear-log and seasonally adjusted ECM, and found no evidence at the 1% level to reject the ECM. The results are not reported here as they are not significantly different to the results reported in Chapter Five.
4. See Endnotes (No.7) of Chapter Five, p. 77.
5. There is some debate on this assumption. There is even a debate on the certainty of the velocity of money in the legitimate economy (see Klovland, 1984; and Hill and Kabin, 1996 for a discussion).
6. In order to reduce the volatility of short-term fluctuations in the estimates, a 4 period centered moving average was constructed.
7. The correct interpretation of Figure 6.2 is important. It must be clear at the outset that the figure does not suggest an alternative time series for the Federal Budget. Rather it should be interpreted as a series of possible positions that may have been attained in any particular year if attempts were made to uncover and tax the cash economy. This is particularly important because these estimates are based on the assumption that taxes are unchanged from those observed throughout the estimation period. If the Federal Budget went into surplus following additional tax revenue from the cash economy, tax rates and the size of the cash economy in subsequent years may have changed. One should therefore regard these as relevant only for any one particular year.

   It is also important to note that uncovering subterranean activity may not necessarily mean that the activity becomes legitimate and from which tax may be collected. In fact it may be the case that when the activity is exposed, the tax obligations make it unprofitable to continue with the activity. The result may be that the individual or business may simply cease undertaking those activities altogether. The consequences for revenue are clear. It is unlikely that calculating the tax gap as is done in Table 6B.1 of Appendix 6B, will give a reasonable indicator of possible tax revenue. The combination of the discouraged effect and the probability of detection may reduce the scope for tax collections enormously.

Appendix 6A

Table 6A.1 Dickey-Fuller Unit Root Tests

Variable Y_t	Level (L) & 1st Difference (D) series	q d	Levels Constant No Trend $\alpha(1)=0$ τ	Constant Trend $\alpha(1)=\alpha(2)=0$ F-test Φ_3
Log(YD)	L	11	1.342	1.053
	D	11	2.974	5.456
Log(C)	L	8	1.476	1.602
	D	8	4.080	9.874
Log(R)	L	10	1.238	2.095
	D	3	4.079	8.952
Log(π)	L	8	1.447	2.422
	D	8	4.774	11.800
Log(E)	L	8	2.095	3.785
	D	9	4.497	10.024
Log(T_{x1})	L	8	2.488	3.134
	D	11	2.603	5.745
Log(T_{x2})	L	8	2.971	4.471
	D	11	4.270	9.075
Log(W)	L	5	1.883	2.372
	D	5	3.796	7.598

Notes: (i) Column 4 has the following Dickey-Fuller specifications:

$$\Delta Y_t = \alpha_0 + \alpha_1 Y_{t-1} + \sum_{i=1}^{q} b_i \Delta Y_{t-i} + \varepsilon_t$$

while Column 5 has the following specifications (where t = time trend)

$$\Delta Y_t = \alpha_0 + \alpha_1 Y_{t-1} + \alpha_2 t + \sum_{i=1}^{d} b_i \Delta Y_{t-i} + \varepsilon_t$$

(ii) Null hypotheses are found at the head of each column. $\alpha(1)=0$ in column 4 is a τ-tests and in column 5, $\alpha(1) = \alpha(2) = 0$ is a unit root tests with non-zero drift (F-test Φ_3). The critical τ-statistic for column 4 is -2.57, and the critical F-test Φ_3 for column 5 is 5.34.

(iii) d and q were chosen as the highest lag from the autocorrelation function of the first differenced series at the 95% confidence interval.

Table 6A.2 Endogeniety Tests

Dependent Variable	Instruments		
$\Delta \ln(Z)$	$\sum_{i=1}^{N} \Delta \ln(Z_{t-i})$, $\sum_{i=1}^{N} \Delta \ln(C_{t-i})$		
	t-statistics[a]		
	N=3	N=4	N=5
$\Delta \ln(T_H)$	-0.048	-0.141	-0.139
$\Delta \ln(T_B)$	0.998	0.595	0.857
$\Delta \ln(YD)$	-0.235	1.591	1.043
$\Delta \ln(W)$	-1.007	-1.299	-1.038
$\Delta \ln(E)$	-0.782	0.968	-1.043

Notes: (a) t statistic on $\Delta \ln(Z)$ when included as an independent variable in equation (6.4).

Table 6A.3 Properties of Residuals

			No Constant, No Trend $[\alpha(1) = 0]$				
e(x)	e(0)	e(1)	e(2)	e(3)	e(4)	e(5)
τ	10.68	7.03	6.49	5.09	5.15	5.48

Notes: (i) e(x) where x indicates the number of lagged terms in the augmented Dickey-Fuller regression.

$$\Delta e_t = \alpha_1 e_{t-1} + \sum_{i=1}^{q} b_i \Delta e_{t-i} + \varepsilon_t$$

(ii) Null hypothesis is found at the head of the table: $\alpha(1)=0$. The critical τ-statistic is 5.028. Phillips and Ouliaris (1990), p. 190.

Appendix 6B

Table 6B.1 Estimates of the Cash Economy in Australia – Business and Households

	Cash Economy (Business) $m 89/90 prices	Cash Economy (Consumer) $m 89/90 prices	Cash Economy (Total) $m 89/90 prices	Cash Economy[a] (Business) (% of GDP)	Cash Economy[a] (Consumer) (% of GDP)	Cash Economy[a] (Total) (% of GDP)	Tax gap (Total) $m 89/90 prices
1978	16324.15	20098.43	36422.58	6.53	8.01	14.54	5664.20
1979	16837.75	21414.07	38251.83	6.39	8.13	14.52	5674.49
1980	18920.67	21976.97	40897.64	7.01	8.15	15.16	6343.34
1981	19643.87	23056.91	42700.79	7.03	8.24	15.27	6963.36
1982	19330.71	22380.23	41710.94	6.95	8.05	15.00	6874.22
1983	17322.24	22610.18	39932.42	6.19	8.04	14.23	6378.42
1984	19654.95	24970.30	44625.25	6.48	8.25	14.73	6977.26
1985	20586.03	26301.21	46887.24	6.53	8.34	14.87	7642.26
1986	21607.92	26581.08	48189.00	6.73	8.27	15.00	8179.88
1987	22123.76	28221.18	50344.94	6.58	8.39	14.97	8665.91
1988	22386.08	29875.66	52261.74	6.39	8.52	14.91	9041.55
1989	24185.88	30571.93	54757.81	6.61	8.37	14.99	9451.31
1990	25795.19	29719.66	55514.85	6.96	8.02	14.98	9643.92
1991	24149.61	28772.49	52922.10	6.63	7.89	14.52	9050.04
1992	23591.26	30013.26	53604.52	6.28	7.99	14.28	8616.53
1993	24368.70	31670.46	56039.16	6.24	8.11	14.35	8768.63
1994	26769.53	33584.78	60354.31	6.53	8.20	14.73	9527.88
1995	28456.79	35203.80	63660.59	6.74	8.33	15.06	10625.90
1996	30753.42	37318.22	68071.63	6.80	8.26	15.06	11600.96
1997	30673.25	38348.39	69021.64	6.34	7.92	14.26	11702.26
1998	32153.66	40615.28	72768.94	6.32	7.99	14.32	12424.41
1999	33691.12	42662.54	76353.67	6.38	8.07	14.44	13312.66

Appendix 6B 137

	Cash Economy (Business) $m 89/90 prices	Cash Economy (Consumer) $m 89/90 prices	Cash Economy (Total) $m 89/90 prices	Cash Economy[a] (Business) (% of GDP)	Cash Economy[a] (Consumer) (% of GDP)	Cash Economy[a] (Total) (% of GDP)	Tax gap (Total) $m 89/90 prices
2000.1[b]	8256.07	10807.89	19063.96	6.30	8.25	14.55	3329.38
2000.2[b]	8295.12	10645.14	18940.26	6.10	7.82	13.92	3310.72
2000.3[b]	7820.70	10176.65	17997.36	5.62	7.31	12.93	3241.44
2000.4[b]	8917.94	10833.46	19751.40	6.14	7.46	13.61	3182.46

Notes: (a) Average quarterly percentage change over the year.
(b) March, June, September and December quarters of 2000 are quarterly estimates only.

7 Measures to Combat Clandestine Activities

The subject of this book has been to investigate the extent by which official statistics are distorted and tax obligations evaded. The earlier chapters demonstrated the adverse implications that arise from a large and volatile underground economy, particularly for public policy. Having said this, many macroeconomists and policy makers have paid little scholarly attention to the underground economy, at least until recently. Reuter (1982) has suggested that many of the paradoxes of recent macroeconomic performances are not the failing theory but data (p. 125). In fact significant distortions to macroeconomic data that are generated from underground economic activity may weaken the effectiveness of policy prescriptions implemented to accommodate changes in economic conditions.

Designing policies that will be effective in reducing participation in the underground economy is a difficult task. This chapter elaborates on the various steps a select group of countries have taken to minimize participation in the underground economy. Although certain strategies have produced some desirable outcomes, the same cannot be said of every strategy. The strategies that have shown some promise in minimizing underground activity are the 'microeconomic' initiatives designed to address specific sectors of the economy, for example, programs targeting the housing construction industry and the payments to sub-contractors. The broader singular reforms put into place to tackle the underground economy appear not to have been as effective. For example, the introduction of the GST in Canada and New Zealand did not deter participation in the underground economy as might have been expected. In fact the evidence suggests that the outcome has probably worsened.

Programs Implemented Abroad

In this chapter we examine how New Zealand, Canada and the United Kingdom have attempted to deal with their underground economies. These three countries have devoted a large number of staff and financial resources in implementing a number of initiatives in the hope of significantly reducing tax evasion. The same three countries also have a common platform of indirect tax collections - the Value Added Tax (VAT) in the United Kingdom and the GST in Canada and New Zealand. Australia now shares a similar tax system with these three countries and it makes sense to study Australia's cash economy in light of their experiences. In particular we will take a closer look at the 'microeconomic' policies that they have implemented in the prospect of using similar initiatives to deal with what appears to be a resilient cash economy in Australia.

United Kingdom

The United Kingdom introduced a 10% VAT in 1973 to replace the Purchase Tax and the Selective Employment Tax. By January 1993 the VAT rate climbed to 15% and has since increased again to 17.5%.[1] In the early days of its introduction the government collected about 10% of its revenue from this tax but by the turn of the century it returned the government about 25% of its total revenue (BRW, 1999).

Has the change in the tax mix affected the size of the underground economy in the UK? Although there are a number of estimates of the size of the underground economy, the research nevertheless shows a consistent upward trend in the volume of illicit activities. Bhattacharyya (1990) finds the introduction of the VAT had little effect on participation in the underground economy. The findings suggest that the year after the VAT's introduction the underground economy had climbed to about 9.5% of GNP from an average of 5% of GNP during the 1960s. Feige (1981) similarly concluded that the underground economy grew throughout 1973-74, and although it declined somewhat after 1974, it remained at levels higher than pre-VAT. Frey and Weck-Hannemann (1983) and Macafee (1980) also arrive at similar conclusions.

Without doubt participating in the underground economy increases a participant's disposable income. For example, employers that participate in the underground economy and avoid detection by paying their employees in cash benefit because they:[2]

- Do not pay National Insurance Contributions (a rate of 12% for those with no occupational pension arrangements);
- Pay less under Pay-As-You-Earn (PAYE) than they would otherwise; and
- Avoid their VAT obligations on undeclared sales.

Similarly employees benefit because by receiving undeclared cash payments some may become eligible for welfare benefits which they wouldn't otherwise if their income had been reported. The Benefit Agency, which oversees the payment to UK welfare recipients, has found that at any one time up to 120,000 people in receipt of these payments are making fraudulent claims (Grabiner, 2000). In most cases these involve the recipient failing to report either their employment or receipt of cash payments. This fraudulent activity has been estimated to cost the government about £450 million annually. The various fraudulent claims that have been detected are reported in Table 7.1. It appears from this that welfare fraud is widespread in the UK.

The strong growth in e-commerce has also heightened Inland Revenue's fears that the opportunities to evade income tax may be rapidly increasing the size of the underground economy in the UK. Governments around the world are concerned with this type of evasion and are actively cooperating by working together to monitor unusually large flows of funds within their own jurisdiction. However it is possible that much of this form of tax evasion is frequent but small-scale evasion that may go undetected. The Inland Revenue has suggested the following reasons why detecting tax evasion through e-commerce can be quite difficult.[3] These include:

- The internet offers anonymity, that is, the person trading on the internet could effectively hide their identity and location from the tax authorities or anybody else for that matter, including the customer;
- The internet allows for easy and possibly undetectable transfer of funds and other assets abroad from the prying eyes of local tax administrators;
- Encryption of documents and financial records could make it extremely difficult for the tax administrator to uncover details of transactions that have not been disclosed to the appropriate tax authorities; and
- The internet provides the ability to hide records on economic transactions in other jurisdiction that make it difficult, possibility for legal reasons, to retrieve.

Table 7.1   Examples of Identified Welfare Fraud

- An unemployed man with family, claiming Jobseeker's Allowance, did a few decorating jobs, cash-in-hand, for neighbours to earn some extra money before Christmas and failed to declare earnings.
- A couple, where the wife worked full-time at a nursing home and her husband claimed Jobseeker's Allowance without reporting her earnings.
- A lone parent claiming income support who was in full-time work as a market trader, while living with someone who was in full-time work.
- A man who worked for a number of employers, using false identities and claiming benefits at the same time.
- A firm of drivers where the employer failed to provide a full list of employees and kept two sets of financial accounts. He also colluded in benefit fraud by allowing employees time to sign on as unemployed.
- A coach company where the employer left out claimants from a list of employees supplied to the Benefits Agency, and falsified dates and wages.
- Visits to 11 firms in the clothing industry found that 106 out of 365 employees had irregular benefit claims. False records were given to the Inland Revenue in several cases, and over £100,000 was assessed in unpaid VAT.
- An agricultural firm where 28 out of 125 employees were wrongfully claiming benefits, and 8 were arrested as illegal immigrants.
- A London based organization of bogus companies specializing in large scale benefits, mortgage and property fraud; importing illegal immigrants; and cocaine dealing. Evidence of over 500 fraudulent benefit claims, worth around £4 million. 50 known cases of identity fraud. Over 40 claims for Child Benefit supported by counterfeit documents.

Source: Grabiner (2000).

As part of its own initiative, Inland Revenue is requiring its staff 'to acquire and develop specific skills to audit' these type of activities as well as being made 'aware of developments in this field to ensure their skills remain commensurate'.[4]

The Inland Revenue has proposed a number of objectives for maintaining a high degree of integrity of the tax system. These have included (i) simplifying tax reporting requirements and obligations; (ii) keeping tax compliance cost low and (iii) dealing with tax evasion very quickly as it arises. In response to (iii) a Task Force was set up in 1999 to make recommendations on ways to deal with the underground economy. The Task Force members were drawn from many government departments including Treasury, Inland Revenue, Customs and Excise and the Department of Social Security and Employment Service. The Task Force's terms of reference required a focus on high risk areas including unregistered businesses, employees participating in the underground economy, those who are claiming social security payments while working and the self employed. The Task Force was headed by Lord Grabiner QC, and was commissioned to report to parliament on its findings and recommendations. Defining the underground economy to include not only unreported legitimate transactions but also criminal activities, the Task Force reported the underground economy in the UK to be a major problem worth billion of pounds a year.

The report tabled in parliament included seventeen recommendations that the UK government is currently considering to implement. The government is also considering introducing data protection laws to protect those citizens who report fraudulent behaviour to the tax authorities or relevant government departments. A suggestion for a US style 'two-strikes and you're out' policy in relation to welfare fraud is also on the table for discussion. The United States policy is to refuse welfare assistance to anyone who has sought refuge from the system more than twice. The report also suggests that there is evidence of a growing number of frauds described as 'Day of the Jackal Fraud' after Frederick Forsyth's thriller in which a character assumes the identity, by birth certificate, of a child who died in their childhood. In Table 7.2 is a list of the Task Force's recommendations. They are grouped into five categories that cover:

(i) incentives, and
(ii) preventative measures
designed to help promote active participation in legitimate activities.
(iii) detection, and
(iv) enforcement
designed to discourage existing participants from continuing to part-take in underground activities; and

(v) publicity
to increase public awareness of the risks and consequences of participating in the underground economy.

Table 7.2   Informal Economy Report: Recommendations

Incentives to Join the Legitimate Economy

- Set up a confidential telephone line to advise people how they can put their affairs in order;
- Extend the existing measures to make it easier for people claiming means-tested benefits and take up legitimate jobs; and
- Increase the help that is given to people when they set up as self-employed.

Prevention

- People should be required to tell the Inland Revenue as soon as they start up in business, not least so that they can be offered early advice, especially about record keeping;
- To combat identity fraud, the procedures for issuing National Insurance numbers should be tightened, in line with the regime already piloted by the Benefits Agency; and
- There should be better controls on the issue and use of birth certificates, to prevent their use of proof of identity by third parties.

Detection

- Consider ways to use information from private sector sources as a cross-check on the details people provide to Departments (such as where they live and whether they have a bank account);
- Give investigators power to make routine 'reverse searches' of the telephone directory to find names and addresses of people who advertise businesses only giving their telephone number;

- Agree on common guidelines for staff about what data sharing is legally permissible and how it should be carried out in practice. There should be a central point of contact to co-ordinate the exercise and monitor its effectiveness; and
- Build on the joint work already started by Department by setting up a specific Government function or line of work, accountable for detecting and investigating businesses in the hidden economy.

Punishment

- Establishing a new statutory offence of fraudulently evading income tax, which would be tried in a magistrate's court. Currently only very large scale offences are prosecuted;
- Requiring people suspected of working while claiming that they are unemployed to attend the Job Centre more frequently, and at unpredictable times, as a condition of receiving their benefit;
- More use should be made of a warning procedure, for example, to employers reasonably suspected of colluding with fraudulent benefit claims, that if they do not clean up their act they will expose themselves to more detailed investigation and possible prosecution;
- If other measures fail to work, considering the option of punishing persistent fraudsters by removing, or heavily reducing, their right to benefit for a specified period; and
- Carrying out research into the sentence imposed for benefit fraud and, in particular, into variation in the sentencing of persistent offenders.

Publicity

- Publicising both the incentives available for people to join the legitimate economy and the risks of staying in, or supporting the informal economy; and
- Testing the use of advertising as a tool for changing public attitudes, insofar as they regard the hidden economy as socially acceptable.

Source: Grabiner (2000).

For those who are active in the underground economy, a number of recommendations were made. These recommendations included:

- Obtaining private sector information which could be used to cross-check income tax returns submitted;
- 'Reverse searches' which involve reverse searching the telephone directory to find names and addresses of individuals who may advertise a business using only a telephone number; and
- Data sharing arrangements amongst departments to help complement cross checking of income tax returns.

A number of these recommendations may not be pursued because they are clearly controversial. For example, the civil liberties group is strongly opposed to the 'reverse charges' recommendation. Data rules currently prohibit these types of searches from taking place.

The recommendations designed to punish those who consistently refuse to 'go straight' and continue to actively engage in underground activities include:

- Trialing offences in a magistrate's court, which up until now only deals with major cases of tax evasion;
- Creating a criminal offence for fraudulent tax evasion;
- Ensuring that those suspected of working in the underground economy and defrauding the welfare system be expected to turn up to the Benefits Agency frequently and at times that are unpredictable; and
- More extensive use made of warnings that alert participants to possible prosecutions if they evade their tax obligations.

However the Task Force rejected outright any amnesty to encourage those who work in the underground economy to come forward. The actions of those who participate in the underground economy disadvantage those who are honest and meet their tax obligations and a general amnesty would be seen to be offering 'a free lunch to those who have not met their responsibility'.

To be effective, sanctions not only have to be publicized, but they also have to be effectively enforced otherwise publicity will do more harm than good. Publicity may sanction activities in the underground economy if it identifies offenders. Although offenders in the UK have their names and details of their offence publicized, its effectiveness has not been documented. If the estimates of the underground economy are anything to go by, publicity appears to have had a negligible effect at least in the long term. For Australia at least, publicity that the cash economy was going to be detected had an immediate impact but more recent data suggests that the impact may fade unless followed by enforcement. Nevertheless it is possible that an effective publicity campaign may succeed in changing social behaviour and therefore contributes to reducing participation in illicit activities over a longer horizon. To be conclusive on this point however requires further research, which until now has lacked considerably.

New Zealand

New Zealand introduced a 10% GST in 1986 that climbed to 12.5% by 1989. With the introduction of the GST came major changes to the marginal tax rate, which in 1986 was reduced from 66% to 48% and reduced again to 33% by 1988. The company tax rate was also reduced to 33%. But how did such a significant change to the tax mix affect the size of the underground economy in New Zealand? The evidence appears to suggest that although the size of the underground economy declined for some time after the introduction of the GST, the underground economy eventually increased to levels above that which existed before the change to the tax system. Giles (1999b, 2000) examined the underground economy in New Zealand before and after the introduction of the GST and suggested that:

- The introduction of the GST was followed by a rapid increase in the size of the underground economy by 2% of GDP until 1988. Between 1988 and 1992 the underground economy reportedly declined by 2.5% of GDP only to see the decline reversed by 1994. By that time the underground economy in New Zealand had grown to levels greater than the pre-GST years;
- Unemployment, inflation, economic growth and government regulation were found to impact significantly on public perceptions of government. In combination these factors encouraged participation in the underground economy;
- Increases in the proportion of indirect taxes relative to direct taxes reduces the underground economy *(but only temporarily)* – emphasis added;
- Decreasing the tax/GDP ratio reduces, but only slightly, the size of the underground economy.

To discourage tax evasion the Inland Revenue Department embarked on a number of strategies to help tackle non-compliance. These strategies included:

- Introducing and ensuring that penalty provisions are more effective in deterring non-compliant behaviour;
- Obtaining and using information from various sources, including government departments, more effectively to identify high risk threats to the tax base;
- Implementing a wide range of compliance initiatives. These initiatives are quite broad and include increasing the number of community visits; improving auditing and intelligence obtained from other departments; training staff and conducting research into all matters relating to non-compliance and fraud. In Table 7.3 is an outline of these compliance initiatives.

Table 7.3   New Zealand's Compliance Improvement Initiatives

- Improving society's compliance attitudes towards tax compliance by promoting to the community the consequences to the evader and to society generally of people cheating on their tax obligations;
- Improving Inland Revenue presence by, for example, co-locating staff with other agencies and enabling staff to work from home in areas where there is no office presence by the department;
- Improving detection capability and investigating the effectiveness of conducting random audits;
- Utilizing intelligence collected from the several customer segments of the department;
- Conducting research into the compliance of immigrants who have English as their second language by testing the extent to which their businesses are included in the tax system;
- Improving staff capability by training new staff and retaining those audit staff with existing experience and by being more competitive in the employment market for these skills.

Source: IRD (1999).

A committee established in 1999 to examine the underground economy in New Zealand made a number of recommendations to parliament to help reduce tax evasion (IRD, 1999). The major recommendations proposed included:

- The Inland Revenue has to increase the credibility of its tax auditing processes by sustained attacks on tax evasion;
- The system of withholding tax should not impose excessive costs on those who are entitled to make deductions. Also every opportunity should be undertaken to increase the efficiency of the existing withholding tax system or to consider a new design;
- Audits should not only target specific types of tax evasion but encompass the wide range of tax evasion possibilities. This approach will not only draw attention to a wide range of taxpayers but make the auditing process more credible;
- Increasing community awareness that the underground economy imposes significant costs to honest taxpayers and legitimate businesses;
- Review the law in relation to non-cash payments and increase awareness of such laws in areas of the community where non-cash transactions are common;
- Assist small business with keeping good records particularly on how to seek good professional advice if the need arises. The Inland Revenue should develop a 'toolkit' for tax agents to use when preparing income tax returns; and
- Working closely with community groups and tax practitioners to develop public awareness campaigns that attempt to improve taxpayer compliance.

Canada

Canada introduced a 7% GST in 1991 to replace the old manufacturer's tax of 13.5%. However in a number of Canadian provinces consumers are required to pay a Provincial Sales Tax (PST) that varies between 0% and 10%. In the three provinces of New Brunswick, Nova Scotia and Newfoundland a Harmonized Sales Tax (HST) rate of 15% is in place. The HST combines the PST with the GST.

Did the introduction of the GST in Canada affect participation in the underground economy? Not surprisingly the answer to this question appears to be no. Revenue Canada admits that while the underground economy is a complex issue to deal with, it requires constant monitoring and attention.

To ensure that the underground economy received constant attention, the government announced in 1993 an Underground Economy Initiative following community perceptions that the underground economy in Canada was growing. A number of surveys undertaken by various organizations between 1994 and 1997 reported an alarmingly large number of Canadians were willing to participate in the underground economy if the opportunity arose. Although publicized, the initiative appeared to have little effect on participation in the underground economy. In 1994 a Canadian television program conducted a poll to measure community attitude towards the underground economy. The results revealed that 58% of callers were willing to participate in the underground economy. In 1997 a Gallup poll suggested that attitudes had worsened, as 73% of respondents would willingly participate in the underground economy in the opportunity did arise.

The Underground Economy Initiative comprised of seven pillars designed not only to ensure the integrity and fairness of the voluntary tax system but also to restore the level playing field that was being undermined by the existence of an underground economy. These seven pillars are listed in Table 7.4. To ensure that Revenue Canada would meet its Compliance Strategy it allocated 200 staff to its non-filers and non-registrants program as well as additional 1,000 staff members to audit small business. About 35% of the staff working with small and medium sized businesses at Revenue Canada are involved in the Underground Economy Initiative.

Several provinces have made separate attempts to deal with the underground economy in Canada. For example, a number of strategies were announced in Quebec's 1997 Provision Budget Papers in an attempt to deal with the underground economy. These included:

- Hire additional personnel as well as facilitate an effective data processing center for the use and exchange of information with other government agencies;
- Accelerate prosecutions and increase fines for tax evasion;
- Deal with the problems of undeclared tips. Each employee is expected to surrender their tips to their employer who is required to withhold 20% to meet Quebec and Federal income tax obligations.

Each employee will be assumed to have received 8% of sales as tips. If an employee remits less than 8% of sales as tips, the employer will nevertheless be required to withhold the equivalent deduction at the source. Employers are compensated for the additional payroll tax they have to pay on tip income by way of a refundable tax credit.

Table 7.4   Canada's Compliance Strategy

- Identification of non-filers and GST non-registrants;
- Special audit teams focused on areas of high non-compliance – such as construction and home renovation, auto sales and repair, jewellery and hospitality;
- Working cooperatively with other federal departments and the provinces to encourage voluntary compliance and combat underground activities;
- Working with key industry groups and professional associations to encourage voluntary compliance;
- Increasing visibility of compliance and enforcement activities by publicizing convictions for tax evasion and conducting community visits;
- Reviewing and acting on referrals from the public; and
- Increasing public awareness of Revenue Canada's voluntary disclosure policy.

Source: CCRA (1998).

The results from this initiative have been:

- Voluntary disclosures have quadrupled since 1993;
- Department staff have visited 160 communities and met with more than 290,000 businesses;
- More than $2.3 billion in additional tax revenue from November 1993 resulting from enforcement activities related to the underground economy. Table 7.5 demonstrates two of many cases of tax evasion which Revenue Canada has detected and publicized;
- The Department has obtained over 480,000 returns from non-filers in 1996/97.

Table 7.5   Selected Cases of Tax Evasion

Case 1: A Canadian taxpayer evaded personal income taxes to an amount of $32,607 and failed to remit payroll deductions for an amount of $70,502. Over a period of three years the same taxpayer failed to enter into the books a number of cheques that were made out in cash to an amount of $1,589,018. The Quebec provincial court first fined the taxpayer $65,214 (or 200% of the tax evaded) plus an 18 month prison sentence. A second sentence added $70,502 to the previous fine and another 18 month prison term while the third conviction added another 18 month goal sentence.

Case 2: A Canadian taxpayer operated an exterior siding and renovation business. Between 1996 and 1997 $20,690 in revenue was not disclosed to the Canadian Customs and Revenue Agency as well as failing to remit $2,470 in GST. The court was told that the same taxpayer failed to issue invoices and on those which were issued the GST was reported separately to make them appear professional. The taxpayer was required to pay more than $11,000 in unpaid taxes, interest and fines.

Source: Case 1: (CCRA, 2001a); Case 2: (CCRA, 2001b).

However according to the Committee that made the recommendations, Revenue Canada has not been as active in the pursuit of subterranean participants as should have been expected. For example Revenue Canada did not (Revenue Canada, 1999):

- Undertake the public awareness campaign which constitutes a major part of one of the seven pillars in the Underground Economy Initiative;
- Undertake research on the impact social marketing may have on voluntary non-compliance;
- Engage in an appropriate number of community visits. In 1995/96 about 60 visits with community groups had been arranged, however, by 1997/98 only 37 community visits had been undertaken. Follow up meetings also declined.

In response to the investigation heralding an apparent lack of action by Revenue Canada, the Department committed to a number of recommendations (Revenue Canada, 1999):

- Examine how Canadian taxpayers respond to their concerns about the underground economy and what they perceive to be the impact on social programs;
- Investigate whether a broad-based advertising campaign could be an effective tool in raising public awareness about the underground economy and what Inland Revenue has done to reduce participation in the underground economy;
- 'Improve and expand its existing communications efforts targeted at specific industry sectors and related consumers';
- After the committee's findings that community visits have declined dramatically, Revenue Canada has agreed to commit itself to increasing community visits and on maintaining relationships that have already been established;
- Collaborate with government departments and other organizations to collate data with that collected by Revenue Canada;
- Revenue Canada will develop an effective sector profile. In other words, auditors investigating certain types of underground economic activity need to have good understanding of the activities that they are auditing as well as the risks the sector posses for non-compliance (see Table 7.6);
- Revenue Canada will increase its record keeping of the Initiative's success.

The report also proposed a number of legislative opportunities that may be used to deter tax evasion. These include (Revenue Canada, 1999):

Reporting Requirements

Requiring construction contractors to report payments made to sub-contractors to the Department. Revenue Canada will use this information to match its records of the sub-contractors tax return. Revenue Canada is hoping to expand this initiative to the housing renovation sector of the economy.

Table 7.6 Housing Construction Industry Initiative

- Revenue Canada and the Canadian Home Builders Association established a working group to address areas of mutual concern;
- Over 13,000 underground economy audits have been completed and $165 million in taxes have been reassessed;
- Additional sources of information including building permits, municipal and provisional licensing, and materials supplied are being used to help identify underground activity;
- A revised GST New Housing Rebate form was first introduced in 1997. As part of the form, owner builders are required to provide information on who did the work and how much was paid;
- The Department participates in home renovation and industry trade shows to raise industry awareness of underground economy issues and to provide consumers with information on the pitfalls of dealing with the underground economy.

Source: CCRA (1998).

Requesting a Re-filing

Revenue Canada could pursue the option of requiring a taxpayer who is suspected of filing a wrong or incorrect tax return to re-file a return. The law allows for doubling of the tax liability as a penalty if the forms are incorrect.

Monetary Penalties

Revenue Canada could consider specifying a monetary penalty for not lodging a tax return after a notice has been issued as well as penalties for poor record and book keeping. Taxpayers with a record of underreporting to be forced to keep onerous records of their sales and purchases.

Reporting Cash Transactions

Although some countries have reporting requirements for cash transactions over a certain amount, Canada only has legislation in place for such transactions that occur within the banking system. It was suggested that the government should establish a centralized agency that investigated suspicious transactions. The approach would help to uncover money laundering which would otherwise go undetected as well as cash sales that go unreported.

Australia

In an address to the Taxation Institute of Australia in 1998, the Australian Tax Commissioner expressed concerns about the state of play in the cash economy, much of which was driven by survey results indicating the cash economy was an accepted practice in the working ethos of many ordinary Australians. One of such surveys found 55% of respondents reporting that a lot of people they knew thought it was OK not to report cash payments. Of more concern to the tax office was that only 31% of respondents agreed that the ATO is doing a good job in keeping the cash economy under control while 48% of respondents disagreed.

The research undertaken by the ATO into taxpayer attitudes was not at all encouraging. Small business reported that the lack of fairness and the complexity of the tax system was a problem that the ATO has to address. Small business raised a number of issues which included (see ATO, 1997): (i) small business lacked trust in the ATO; (ii) ATO staff were seen as 'threatening, uncommunicative and lacking empathy'; (iii) ATO placed unrealistic expectations on businesses; (iv) penalties were too heavy; (v) there was no recognition of good behaviour; and (vi) the taxpayer is generally presumed to be guilty. Although the ordinary taxpayer shared much of these concerns, it was with the general complexity of the (old) tax system that they were most unhappy about.

After heightened community concerns that the underground economy in Australia was growing the Tax Commissioner established a Cash Economy Task Force in 1996. The role of the Task Force was to examine closely what motivates participation in the cash economy and to make recommendations to the Commissioner on how to improve tax compliance.

The ATO had a number of initiatives in place at the time to deter activities in the cash economy. These included (ATO, 1997):

- Record keeping programs that educate businesses in the ways to keep good records;
- A range of audit programs to investigate those suspected of tax evasion;

- A special investigation program designed to investigate illegal activities.

After the first meeting of the Cash Economy Task Force, the following recommendations were made to supplement these existing initiatives (ATO, 1999).

- To research the motivating factors and structural issues relating to the cash economy in conjunction with industry, community groups and tax practitioners;
- Increase community awareness of the consequences of a growing cash economy particularly on businesses;
- Evaluate policy proposals that would increase the ATO's ability to deal more effectively with the cash economy;
- Equipping the staff at the ATO with the necessary skills to contribute effectively to compliance matters which deal specifically with the cash economy.

In response to these recommendations, the Commissioner of Taxation announced (ATO, 1998c):

- Redeployment of field resources – increasing appropriate staff to deal with compliance issues from 300 to 900. Each of these staff are also engaged in giving advice to new businesses whether it be with regards to record keeping or other tax related matters;
- Develop regional as well as national projects that are targeted at high risk cash industries;
- The commencement of consultations with industry and community groups to get feedback on the factors that would contribute to the cash economy;
- A better integration of ATO activities and the department responsible for social security assistance;
- A broadening of the Task Force membership to include industry and community groups.

The Cash Economy Task Force reconvened and published its second report in 1998. The key recommendations are summarized below (ATO, 1998b):

Understanding compliance
- The ATO needs to develop a greater understanding of the issues that discourage compliance and particularly the costs such participation may have on the community and businesses;
- The ATO undertake more research of industry specific compliance problems so that a strategy may be implemented to circumvent such practices;
- The ATO increase its presence in high-risk cash industries by offering more support.

Building Partnerships
- The Task Force recommended integrating the 'compliance model' initiatives with the principles of the Taxpayer's Charter. The 'compliance model' promotes a hierarchical approach to administering taxpayer obligations by attempting to maximize voluntary compliance yet maintaining a favourable community attitude towards strong deterrence policies. The Taxpayers' Charter is the result of ATO consultations with industry practitioners, community groups and government departments designed to improve the relationship between the ATO and the taxpayer. The objective of the charter is to ensure that taxpayer's legal rights are administered under the law and that the ATO has an obligation to assist the taxpayers in tax related matters that may arise for the taxpayer from time to time. In doing so the Charter is designed to increase taxpayer awareness of their legal rights and obligations as well as an understanding of the services the ATO is capable of delivering as assistance to the taxpayer. It is hoped that such a strategy would increase voluntary compliance and reduce the cost of heavy monitoring;
- Increase community confidence by treating taxpayers in a way they deserve and according to their own particular circumstances. The Task Force sees this as the most appropriate long-term solution to changing taxpayer behaviour;
- The Task Force cautions the use of an educational campaign until an extensive market research is undertaken.

Encouraging and supporting compliance
- The ATO should identify the factors that promote voluntary compliance;
- Allowing amnesties, introducing less stringent tax return requirements, rewarding compliant taxpayers and promoting good record keeping;
- The ATO should reduce the reporting burden, for example, differential record keeping requirements, while also rewarding good compliance and manage poor complying taxpayers.

Enforcing compliance
- The ATO introduce on-the-spot fines for those who do not keep adequate records. The ATO to take every opportunity to assist the taxpayer in complying with their tax obligations before imposing heavy penalties. There should be an adjustment of penalties for those who have a good compliance history, unless of course the offence is serious;
- Impose non-financial sanctions that educate or support the offender. In high-risk areas, the ATO might prescribe onerous reporting requirements;
- The ATO to consider using industry benchmarks as base default assessment for compiling the non-compliant taxpayer's obligations.

As part of the Cash Economy Initiative the ATO has introduced real time reviews in a number of industries including the building/construction and the restaurant/cafe industries. The ATO would frequently, but irregularly, visit these businesses to ensure that good records are being kept. During the review process the ATO would collect information to establish its benchmark ratios similar to those given in Table 6.1. These ratios are used by the ATO to give a first impression as to whether the business is likely to be non-compliant. Depending on whether there is a large discrepancy between the ratio constructed from the business's records and these benchmarks, the ATO would recommend follow up visits and extend the review period.

The ATO chose a number of industries for its Cash Economy Project. These included: (i) building and construction; (ii) clothing; (iii) fruit and vegetables; (iv) prescribed computer goods; (v) restaurants and cafes; and (vi) taxis. The Cash Economy Task Force recommended the ATO's industry initiatives as the most effective way to ensure taxpayer compliance.

The advantages of an industry approach is that there is a greater possibility for improved networking that could develop and foster greater taxpayer compliance in the community. Below we provide the findings for each of the Cash Economy Initiatives for these selected industries.

Building and Construction

The ATO undertook field visits to building sites with the objective to increasing its direct contact with the major payers and payees in order to help establish an external database that could be used to cross check particular tax returns. This initiative helped to uncover a number of undesirable practices in the building and construction industry (see ATO, 1998b):

- A number of workers in the industry did not have tax file numbers;
- There was a substantial number of tax returns that had not been lodged. The ATO detected one sub-contractor who had not lodged their tax return for eight years;
- Cash transactions were not properly recorded;
- There was a number of failures by those in the building industry who did not remit or deduct withholdings under the Prescribed Payments System (PPS);
- There was evidence of cheques being cashed in licensed pubs to avoid them appearing in business records.

Clothing Industry

Before the introduction of the Reportable Payments System (RPS) in the clothing industry, a number of audits revealed that tax evasion was happening on a wide scale. With the introduction of the RPS the ATO has uncovered a number of tax evasion schemes including false invoicing. The clothing industry in Australia was found to involve multi-stages of production involving both formal and informal occupational practices. Many of these stages of production appeared tied together with loose contractual agreements particularly with the more informal sector of the economy. The informal sector is characterized by a large number of home based production typically paid in cash. The clothing industry was found to exhibit the following characteristics (ATO, 1998b):

- That much of the work undertaken is performed at home (home-based production);

- The production process is very labour intensive and very little capital equipment is required;
- There is typically exploitation of outworkers that generally have low employment opportunities elsewhere;
- There are often a large number of fraudulent Social Security claims amongst outworkers;
- Very low levels of cooperation with government regulation; and
- Cultural factors which may include poor language skills.

Although these characteristics vary widely, they clearly highlight the fact that cash economy drivers are many and complex. The findings suggest that sector specific policies targeted at the cash economy are likely to be most efficient in reducing tax evasion than is a broad and singular reform. In fact attempts to introduce broad (tax) reforms both in Australia and abroad have been met with little success.

Restaurants and Cafes and Fruit and Vegetables

The Prescribed Payments System was introduced in the Fruit and Vegetable industry in 1997. The ATO had since undertaken over 1,000 visits to businesses in the industry including green grocers, wholesales and growers. The ATO was happy with the improvement in record keeping but there was still some concern about the volume of cash payments that were taking place.

In the Restaurant and Cafe industry the ATO implemented a three month trial of real time interviews. The owner/operators were required to keep records which the ATO would assess using the financial ratios they had constructed for that industry. The piloted study produced some good results. It increased reported sales by 14.85% or an equivalent of $45,000 per taxpayer per year. Of the sample that was under investigation, 44% had shown improvements in their sales, possibly due to the fact their records were being constantly monitored, and where appropriate, cash counts would be made to match records with till tape records.

Prescribed Computer Goods

In response to a large number of complaints by businesses that there was widespread sales tax evasion in the personal computer industry, the ATO increased its field presence and fined offenders quickly so that the message gets out that sales tax evaders will be detected and prosecuted. When it became clear that sales tax evasion in the computer industry was extensive, the project was given a high priority. The federal government in 1997 allocated additional funding for the ATO to help eliminate sales tax evasion in the industry. After extensive audits had been undertaken many income tax returns were adjusted upwards, refunds were withheld and penalties imposed that reaped the ATO approximately $20 million.

Taxis

The ATO undertook a Taxi Industry Project in 1994 with an objective of developing a tax collection system for taxi drivers, decrease non-disclosure of taxi income and to increase lodgement of tax returns. The ATO has increased its presence in the industry by offering a number of educational strategies that have included seminars, articles in relevant magazines, and distribution of flyers. The Taxi Industry Project delivered some benefits, namely, (i) a $53.2 million increase in taxable income; (ii) a $9.06 million increase in tax being assessed; and (iii) a $2.67 million increase in penalties and interest. Almost 7,000 taxi operators and taxi drivers were reviewed and a number of annual benchmarks were established (takings per kilometre). When a taxi driver had not kept adequate records these benchmarks could be used to determine the amount of tax obligations that taxi driver is required to meet.

Policy Prescriptions

There is no quick fix strategy for reducing the size of the cash or underground economy. The CETF was set up to assist the ATO to come to terms with the motives, consequences and possible strategies to deal with the cash economy. The propositions were never singular but dependent on the type of activities taking place. The Task Force also stressed the importance of the Taxpayer's Charter in facilitating a better 'relationship with the community based on mutual respect and trust'.

The Task Force adapted the work of Ayres and Braithwaite (1992) on strategies for regulation and Braithwaite (1998) on trust norms to develop a compliance model to complement the ATO's Taxpayer's charter. The model has multiple tiers each designed to reduce tax evasion by dishonest taxpayers. In the first instance the ATO's strategy is to encourage self-compliance through means such as education and ATO support. If this approach appears not to work then various escalating enforcement strategies are pursued in order to produce compliant behaviour.

The main principles of the compliance model are as follows:

- To develop an understanding of taxpayer behaviour;
- To establish strong community partnerships which will be on-going;
- To give the ATO the necessary flexibility to not only support compliant behaviour but also to encourage a strong compliant attitude among the taxpaying community;
- To develop more options to enforce tax compliance on those who consistently choose not to comply.

Below is a further list of strategies that may be adopted to help reduce tax evasion.

Reducing the Tax Burden

The tax burden is by far the major factor fostering participation in the underground economy. Broadening the tax base to lower marginal tax rates may reduce the incentive to go underground.

Reporting Requirements

Although there is a great need of data to help in the auditing processes, there is also a need to alleviate businesses of heavy reporting requirements that at times may motivate them to participate in the underground economy. Simplifying the administration of the various taxes that businesses and individuals are required to report may play some part in reducing participation in the underground economy.

Targeting a Low Inflation Rate

Inflation was suggested to offer a motive for participating in the underground economy. Polices designed to maintain moderate rates of inflation are arguably an effective way to reduce the influx of new participants in the underground economy.

Reducing the Appeal of Welfare Benefits

Welfare benefits were argued to provide an incentive to work underground particularly by those who may be in receipt of low income. Several cases of welfare benefit fraud have been identified in Australia and abroad to corroborate this conclusion. Therefore it is important that the welfare benefit system does not ignite enthusiasm for working in the underground economy. It is important that closer monitoring and constant surveillance of welfare recipients is undertaken.

Targeting Most Active Industries

There should be a greater emphasis on targeting specific industries that pose a high risk of tax evasion although more research needs to be undertaken to identify these industries. The results of Chapter Six suggest that the services and housing construction industries in Australia need urgent attention. However the services sector is too broad to tackle and specific high-risk sectors of this industry need to be identified and given priorities.

Education Campaigns

The Cash Economy Task Force recommended 'the ATO ensure that key cash economy messages are well targeted to generated and sustain community support for the ATO'. Thurman, St John and Riggs (1984) caution the use of this approach because it may encourage the individual to rationalise other ways of neutralizing their guilt when evading taxes. An individual may do this in a number of ways (see ATO 1998b):

- *Denial of responsibility* The individual regards the adverse consequences arising from the cash economy to be the result of others, who could even possibly be big players in the cash economy;
- *Denial of injury* The individual disagrees that their activity could have adverse consequences on others. In fact the person may rationalize their actions by arguing that without their services the community may pay a higher price;

- *Denial of victim* The individual accepts the adverse consequences their actions may have on the community but believes that the victims deserve it;
- *Condemnation of condemners* The individual believes that the law, the law-makers and law enforcers are to blame for an unjust system which burdens the community at large. The individual believes that the community should not succumb to these laws and evade if possible;
- *Appeal to higher loyalties* The individual justifies their action as the result of 'non-conventional social order'. The individual believes that similar and across the board behaviour justifies their actions;
- *Metaphor of the ledger* The individual contemplating evading their tax obligations believes that their actions, although they may be bad, are not reflective of their true and good nature. The individual regards these as temporary deviations from otherwise good behaviour;
- *Defence of necessity* The individual justifies their actions as the result of personal circumstances that would not have made them non-compliant had they not existed.

Encouraging and Supporting Compliance

Acknowledging good compliance by means such as (ATO, 1998b):

- a letter thanking those businesses who have participated in the cash economy initiatives;
- follow-up contact with taxpayers who have been visited by the ATO thanking them for their efforts;
- offers to help businesses in their record keeping or any other tax related matters.

Although this has been suggested as significant step in motivating voluntary compliance, it is very doubtful that such a strategy will play anything other than a small role in reducing the size of the cash economy in Australia. Although education has benefits to offer, relying on this strategy alone will fail to deliver results.

Industry Self-Regulation

Promoting industry self-regulation may provide the right impetus to reducing industry specific tax evasion. In fact the ATO encourages industry groups to come up their own solution to resolving the cash economy problem that affects them directly. The ATO has offered to assist and support any initiative that will help reduce activities in the cash economy (see ATO, 1998b). In Table 7.7 is one such example of industry self-regulation that is taking place in one small part of the clothing industry.

Table 7.7   Self-Regulation in the Clothing Industry

Case Study:
The Clothing Industry and the Indo Chinese Cooperative

Springvale Indo Chinese Mutual Assistance Association proposed a clothing cooperative to help combat the low wages being paid to the Indo Chinese workers by clothing manufacturers. Their plan is to ensure that wholesalers directly negotiate with the cooperative that would distribute work to its members. The objective is to dismantle the informal structure where a number of 'middlemen' organise work and exploit workers by offering them low wages. The cooperative hopes that this will ensure that employee's rights are respected and they are paid according to the law.

The CETF has recommended to the ATO that it investigate avenues where such industry self-regulation could be implemented to tackle high-risk cash industries.

Source: ATO (1998b).

Tougher Enforcement

The introduction of the GST in Australia was accompanied by an effective publicity campaign that the cash economy was going to be detected and offenders prosecuted. Even before the introduction of the GST the size of the cash economy declined considerably. In fact the sharp decline in the size of the cash economy occurred in the absence of a sharp decline in legitimate activities. The threat of tougher enforcement was enough to stem the growing activities that were taking place. Therefore the tax office needs to take a tougher stand on tax evasion and follow through by effective enforcement so as to ensure its credibility is not undermined. Otherwise 'talk and no action' will encourage greater participation in the underground economy.

Building Information Databases

There is a great need for better informational databases that tax office staff could use to cross check income tax returns for discrepancies. The tax office may need to provide the resources to ensure that these are collected accurately and to limit the reporting burden that businesses are constantly faced with.

Publicity

The CETF recommended that the ATO should publicize names of individuals who have evaded their tax obligations. It suggested that the ATO could publicize the name of serious offenders in its annual report submitted to parliament. Naming offenders may act a deterrent from participating in the underground economy although evidence abroad suggests that this has had a limited effect.

Notes

1 There is however a number of goods that are still taxed between 4% and 7% while others are 'zero rated' (a zero tax rate applies). For example, domestic fuel is taxed at 5% while postal services, lotteries, trade unions, professional bodies, fund-raising and cultural services are 'zero rated'.
2 Grabiner (2000).
3 IR (1999).
4 IR (1999).

8 Concluding Remarks

The sparse academic discussion on the cash economy in Australia highlights what appears to be little concern on the quality of economic data. Generally training in quantitative economics revolves around analysis of data either using established quantitative tools or more recently developed approaches. Yet very little time is spent, if at all, understanding data collection. Consequently many economists are molded into a mindset which is more often skeptical about failing theory rather than distortions in the data. This book highlights how important it is to recognize data distortions when modeling economic phenomena. The underground (or cash) economy, at least in Australia, has proven to distort significantly the size of national output as well as the swings in the business cycle.

This book has attempted to address three separate issues – (i) the growth of currency in light of growing currency substitutes, (ii) the motives and consequences of participating in the underground economy and (iii) household and business contributions to the overall size of Australia's cash economy.

A review of the literature gave rise to some concern about the quality of the many estimates of the underground economy abroad. It appeared that the various methodologies produced a large number of inconsistencies in the estimates, even for the one country at a given time. A closer look at the interpretations given to the underground economy in Chapter Two revealed a large inconsistency in the activities defined to be taking place. We argued that the underground economy should be viewed as a subset of legitimate activity that is not observed or measured, and, which should be included in the measure of national output. This meant that many activities, defined as criminal, do-it-yourself or other non-market activities, are omitted from the definition of the underground economy. Many of the estimates abroad have used various combinations of criminal, do-it-yourself and non-market activities in defining the underground economy and without doubt have generated what appear to be conflicting estimates. Needless to say, some methodologies are not well suited for estimating the size of the underground economy and as expected these estimates have also compounded the problem.

Chapter Four examined the motives for participating in the underground economy and demonstrated the complex psychology that motivates participation. However an understanding of these motives is extremely important is helping to develop strategies to combat participation, which in Australia appears to be quite significant.

Several factors have been suggested to encourage participation, the most common is the tax burden. Identifying the motives as either economic or institutional helps determine what may change participation over time. We argued that the economic factors, such as the tax burden and welfare benefits, change the composition of the underground economy over time and generate business cycle fluctuations, while the institutional motives, including attitude towards the government and government regulations, tend not to change over time. We argued that the institutional motives may be discouraged by an education campaign, but the economic motives are best dealt with by more effective enforcement.

With a clear definition of what distinguishes the underground economy from the cash economy, a time series estimate of the size of the cash economy in Australia was produced in Chapter Five. We argued that the use of currency was the best medium of exchange to help avoid detection of income earrings from the tax authorities. Consequently the estimate of the cash economy for Australia was derived from modeling currency demand and measuring the excess sensitivity of the two major motives fueling activity in this sector. The two major motives are individual's desire to reduce their tax obligations and to protect their existing welfare entitlements. Our results suggest that many Australians have been actively participating in the cash economy even after the introduction of the GST.

Naturally once participation takes effect, there are a number of consequences that may arise and these were discussed in the second half of Chapter Four. A number of the consequences were identified and they include: the decline in tax revenue, unfair price competition, business cycle distortions, and distortions in economic and social data. The recent publicity on the cash economy in Australia has centered specifically on the loss of tax revenue. Although such concerns are justified on the grounds that they affect the availability and quality of public goods and services, the concern for data quality and the business cycle are just as important, but have been spared little attention.

The business cycle is an essential measure of the economy's dynamic path. Activities that affect the measurement of the data will adversely influence the gauge most commonly used to measure the future path of the economy. Consequently any measurement error in the national accounts will most certainly impact on the nature of the business cycle in general. Having estimated the size of the cash economy two interesting results about the business cycle characteristics of the cash economy and its relationship with the legitimate economy came to light. First, shocks in the legitimate economy induced both an income and substitution effect via changes in income and employment and the former affect was found to dominate the latter. Second, and equally interesting, a significant and volatile cash economy was shown to have adverse implications for the nature of the business cycle in Australia, namely that the existence of a non-negligible underground economy generated more volatile business cycles.

The cash economy in Australia has shown much resilience to government attempts to curb back its size. Measuring on average about 15% of GDP since the late 1970s suggests that many Australians have been actively engaging in the cash economy and it appears that these activities have been entrenched in their working ethics. Tax reform in Australia appears to have had a more negligible impact on the cash economy than in most other economies abroad that embraced similar changes to their tax system. In the quarter leading up to the introduction of the GST the cash economy declined by more than 1.5% of GDP to 13.9% of GDP. The decline continued through to September 2000 (12.9% of GDP) but by December 2000 the cash economy had crept back to 13.6% of GDP. The cash economy in Australia appears to have been resilient to these recent tax changes.

What is of more concern is the fact that unless specific strategies are adopted to deter such participation, these activities will continue to further deprive the government of the much need tax revenue for funding public works and services. Not only are the actions of these participants reducing the size of the tax base, but they are also distorting the quality of national accounts data which the Australian Bureau of Statistics collect and government policymakers use to gauge their policies. What appears to be limiting the provision of public works and services appears also to be affecting the efficiency of public (social) policies that are designed to complement such government expenditure.

There is no escape either for the honest business community who have to compete with those who are engaging in the cash economy. Honest businesses, particularly small business, have to battle against unfair price competition from illegitimate competitors who face significantly lower costs because of tax evasion. The outcome may be a significant rise in small business closures and bankruptcies as well as a growth in subterranean business activity particularly by those businesses that fear the threat of closure.

Governments around the world have used various attempts to stem activities taking place in the cash economy. Many have reformed their tax system or social security systems in the hope that it would discourage participation in the underground economy. Unfortunately such policies have been met with little success. New Zealand, Canada and the United Kingdom introduced changes to their tax system in expectation that they would net a significant part of the cash economy. Their expectations were far from fulfilled. In each of these countries, not only did reforms fail to deliver an increase in tax revenue from the cash economy as had been expected, it appears that the cash economy in each of these three countries has grown since. The Australian government had similar expectations about the success of its the tax reform package. The results of Chapter Five suggest that although early reaction to the introduction of the new tax system dispelled some activities in the cash economy, the effect appeared to have been only transitory. After only a few months from the introduction of the GST, there were signs that the fall in activities in the cash economy had halted and some signs that it may rise again.

In Chapter Six we estimated the contributions by business and households in the cash economy since the late 1970s to determine whether the government's expectations that businesses are the major contributors is correct. The results suggest that over half the cash economy was driven by household participation rather than business participation, contrary to what the government believed. Consumer transactions were found to be more stable as a percentage of GDP than business transactions. In fact the business cycle for the cash economy was essentially driven by illicit business transactions much the same way the legitimate business cycle moves to swings in investment. The findings that the household sector dominates have a serious implication for the success of the new tax system. The design of the new tax system for dealing with the cash economy was based essentially on the premise that the vast majority of unrecorded activities was the result of tax evasion in the business sector. This motivated the introduction of the ABN and the rules for withholding taxes from businesses without this number.

By simulating a number of tax policy changes we found that fiscal policy appears to effect participation to a greater extent after the GST than before, possibly because the distribution between direct and indirect taxes has changed. On this evidence we argue that irresponsible fiscal measures may trigger large changes in the cash economy than was the case under the old tax system.

A summary of the results of Chapter Six include:

- Wage and salary earners were found to participate more actively in the cash economy than businesses. This result challenges the earlier assumptions that 'legitimate' businesses were the major participants in the cash economy. Wage and salary earners engaging in subterranean activities were found to be contributing 55% of the total cash economy (or 8.5% of GDP), while businesses were contributing the remaining 45% (or 6.5% of GDP). The implications of these finding are serious. It suggests that tax reform is unlikely to have a significant effect on the cash economy in the near future because the changes to the tax system were not designed to catch wage and salary participation in the cash economy;
- Of all businesses that participate in the cash economy, small businesses appear to be more active in the cash economy than larger businesses. Of the small businesses, the services and construction industry are the largest contributor to the cash economy. Contrary to public perception portrayed by the media that the transport sector was a major player in the cash economy, this sector is found to be one of the smallest contributors in this study. In the months leading up to the GST, taxi drivers were frequently the subject of discussion on tax avoidance and evasion. These results suggest the construction industry alone was failing to report at least five times more income than was undisclosed to the tax office by the transport industry (including taxi drivers);
- By measuring the responsiveness to changes in taxes on participation it was possible to provide a ranking of industry contributions to illicit activities. Our results suggest that not only do small businesses account for most of business transactions taking place in the cash economy but the services and the housing construction sectors rank as the largest contributors, with NSW harboring much of these activities and South Australia the least. With the availability of these rankings, it is possible to optimize government efforts used to fight growing non-compliance. Not only will this increase the likelihood of success but it

may mean that the size of the cash economy can be reduced to low levels much sooner.

In Chapter Seven we examined some of the strategies that have been adopted in a select group of countries that have undertaken tax reforms similar to those recently introduced in Australia. New Zealand, Canada and the United Kingdom have implemented a number of strategies that deal with incentives and prevention. The establishment of the CETF in Australia has been to identify the right mix of these strategies in the hope of reducing such activities. A 'one-size-fits all' approach is unlikely to deliver any significant results. The CETF's links with industry partners and government departments may provide the right mix of players for understanding and tackling the underground economy in Australia. This seems to be a better approach than trying to achieve the same results by a single reform process, such as was expected from the recent changes to the tax system.

The book's findings have a number of implications for the government, the ATO, the financial markets and honest tax payers who bear the burden of higher taxes that subsidize those who use government goods and services but do not financially contribute to them. The evidence presented in these chapters suggests quite clearly that Australia's new tax system has failed in its attempt to significantly reduce the size of the cash economy. The cash economy in Australia appears entrenched in the working ethos of many ordinary Australians and specific polices to tackle the cash economy may be necessary to reduce participation. It is important then that policymakers and government take seriously the issues relating to the cash economy by considering the rules, regulation, taxes and welfare benefits which have sparked the enthusiasm for these activities and to pursue policies to combat these areas of growing non-compliance.

Bibliography

Akaike, H. (1981), 'Likelihood of a Model and Information Criteria', *Journal of Econometrics*, vol. 16, pp. 3-14.

Australian Bureau of Statistics (ABS) (1990), *Australian National Accounts- Concepts, Sources and Methods*, Catalogue No. 5216.0, Commonwealth Government Printer, Canberra.

Australian Bureau of Statistics (ABS) (1998), *Upgraded National Accounts Information Paper*, Catalogue No. 52530.0, Commonwealth Government Printers, Canberra.

Australian Competition and Consumer Commission (ACCC) (2000), *Debit and Credit Card Schemes in Australia - A Study of Interchange Fees and Access*, a joint publication with the Reserve Bank of Australia, October.

Australian Taxation Office (ATO) *Taxation Statistics*, annual editions (1982 to 1999).

Australian Taxation Office (ATO) (1997), *Cash Economy Report – Improving Tax Compliance in the Cash Economy*, Cash Economy Task Force Report, Canberra.

Australian Taxation Office (ATO) (1998), *Benchmarks Established to Assist Cash Industries*, Cash Economy Media Release, ATO Publication, Canberra.

Australian Taxation Office (ATO) (1998a), *The State of Play Five Years On*, Address to Taxation Institute of Australia, Victorian Division, by Tax Commissioner Michael Carmody, February, ATO Publication, Canberra.

Australian Taxation Office (ATO) (1998b), *Improving Tax Compliance in the Cash Economy*, April, ATO Publication, Canberra.

Australian Taxation Office (ATO) (1998c), *Commissioner's Response to The Cash Economy Task Force Recommendations* (web-site: http://www.ato.gov.au), Canberra.

Ayres, I. and Braithwaite, J. (1992), *Responsive Regulation, Transcending the Deregulation Debate*, Oxford University Press, New York, pp. 3-53.

Bajada, C. (2001), 'An Examination of the Statistical Discrepancy and Private Investment Expenditure', *Journal of Applied Economics*, vol. 4, no. 1, May, pp. 27-61.

Barthelemy, P. (1988), 'The Macroeconomic Estimates of the Hidden Economy: A Critical Analysis', *Review of Income and Wealth*, vol. 34, no. 2, pp. 183-208.

Baumol, W.J., and Tobin. J. (1989), 'The Optimal Cash Balance Proposition: Maurice Allais' Priority', *Journal of Economic Literature*, vol. 27, pp. 1160-2.

Baxter, M. and King, R. (1995), 'Measuring Business Cycles: Approximate Band Pass Filters for Economic Time Series', *NBER Working Paper Series*, No. 5022.
Berger, S. (1986), 'The Unrecorded Economy: Concepts, Approach and Preliminary Estimates for Canada 1981', *Canadian Statistical Review*, Statistics Canada, Cat 11-003E.
Bhattacharyya, D.K. (1990), 'An Econometric Method of Estimating the Hidden Economy, United Kingdom (1960-1984): Estimates and Tests', *The Economic Journal*, vol. 100, September, pp. 703-17.
Blades, D. (1982), 'The Hidden Economy and the National Accounts', *OECD Occasional Studies*, Paris, pp. 28-44.
Blades, D. (1983), 'Crime: What Should Be Recorded in the National Accounts and What Difference Would it Make', *OECD Occasional Studies*, Paris, pp. 45-58.
Boehm, E.A. and Liew, W.T. (1994), 'A Review of Australia's Recent Business Cycle Experiences and a Forecast Length of the Current Expansion', *The Australian Economic Review*, 4th Quarter, pp. 34-56.
Braithwaite, V. (1998), 'Communal and Exchange Trust Norms, Their Value and Relevance to Institutional Trust', in Braithwaite, V. and Levi, M. (1998), pp. 46-74.
Braithwaite, V. and Levi, M. (1998), *Trust and Governance*, New York: Russel Sage.
Brandstaetter, H. and Guth, W. (1994), *Essays on Economic Psychology*, Berlin: Springer, Germany.
Breusch, T.S. and Pagan, A.R. (1979), A Simple Test for Heteroscedasticity and Random Coefficient Variation', *Econometrica*, vol. 47, pp. 1287-94.
Bry, G. and Boschan, C. (1971), *Cyclical Analysis of Time Series: Selected Procedures and Computer Programs*, NBER, New York.
Burns, A.F. and Mitchell, W. (1947), *Measuring Business Cycles*, NBER Studies in Business Cycles, No. 2, New York.
Business Review Weekly (BRW) (1999), 'Vat '73 Ain't What It Used To Be' July 1999, pp. 49-52.
Business Review Weekly (BRW) (2000), 'Why the GST is Good news for the Black Economy', June 2000, pp. 10, 68-76.
Cagan, P. (1958), 'The Demand for Currency Relative to the Total Money Supply', *Journal of Political Economy*, vol. 66, August, pp. 303-28.
Canadian Customs and Revenue Agency (CCRA) (1988), 'Revenue Canada's Underground Economy Initiative', *Underground Economy Initiative (web-site)*, February, 1998.
Canadian Customs and Revenue Agency (CCRA) (2001a), 'Laval Accountant Fined for Tax Evasion', *Tax Evasion Prosecutions (web-site)*, January 2000.
Canadian Customs and Revenue Agency (CCRA) (2001b), 'Regina Man Fined $5,012 for Tax Evasion', *Tax Evasion Prosecutions (web-site)*, February 2000.

Canadian Customs and Revenue Agency (CCRA) (2001c), 'Local Pub Served Fine for Tax Evasion, *Tax Evasion Prosecutions (web-site)*, March 2000.

Carl, P.S. and Witte, A.D. (1982), *Beating the System*, Auburn House Publishing, Boston.

Carson, C.S. (1984), 'The Underground Economy: An Introduction', *Survey of Current Business*, vol. 64, no. 5, pp. 21-37.

Carson, C.S. (1984a), 'The Underground Economy: An Introduction', *Survey of Current Business*, vol. 64, no. 7, pp. 106-17.

Carter, M. (1984), 'Issues in the Hidden Economy - A Survey', *Economic Record*, vol. 60, no. 170, pp. 209-21.

Cebula, R.J., (1997), 'An Empirical Analysis of the Impact of Government Tax and Auditing Policies on the Size of the Underground Economy: The Case of the United States, 1993-94', *American Journal of Economics and Sociology*, vol. 56, no. 2, pp. 173-85.

CENSIS (1976), 'L'occupazione occultra-caratteristiche della partecipazione al lavoro in Italia', cited in Frey, B.S. and Pommerehne, W.W. (1984), *Review of Income and Wealth*, vol. 30, no. 1, pp. 1-23.

Collins, D.J. and Lapsley, H.M. (1991), *Estimating the Economic Costs of Drug Abuse in Australia*, Department of Community Health Services, Canberra, Australia.

Commercial Bank of Australia (CBA) (1980), 'The Underground Economy in Australia,' *CBA Economic Review*, September, pp. 8-12.

Contini, B. (1981), 'Labour Market Segmentation and the Development of the Parallel Economy – The Italian Experience', *Oxford Economic Papers*, vol. 33, no. 3, pp. 401-12.

Cover, J. (1992), 'Asymmetry Effects of Positive and Negative Money Supply Shocks', *Quarterly Journal of Economics*, vol. 107, pp. 1261-82.

Cowell, F.A. (1990), *Cheating the Government*, Cambridge, Mass., MIT Press.

Cox, D. (1984), 'Raising Revenue in the Underground Economy', *National Tax Journal*, vol. 37, no. 3, pp. 283-88.

De Janso, P.E. (1961), 'The Statistical Discrepancy in the National Accounts Revisited', *Econometrica*, vol. 29, no. 3, pp. 427-29.

De Gijsel, P. (1984), 'Okonomische Theorie des Schwarzarbeitsangebots und der Mekrfachbeschaftigung', in Schneider, F. and Enste. D.H. (2000).

De Grazia, R. (1982), 'Clandestine Employment: A Problem of Our Times', in Tanzi, V. (1982), pp. 29-44.

Diebold, F.X. and Rudebusch, G.D. (1989), 'Long Memory and Persistence in Aggregate Output', *Journal of Monetary Economics*, vol. 24, pp. 189-209.

Dilnot, A., and Morris C.N. (1981), 'What Do We Know About the Black Economy in the United Kingdom?', *Fiscal Studies*, vol. 2, pp. 58-73.

Domain, D.L. and Louton, D.A. (1995), 'Business Cycle Asymmetry and the Stock Market', *The Quarterly Review of Economics and Finance*, vol. 35, no. 4, pp. 451-66.

Durbin, J., and Watson, G.S. (1951), 'Testing for Serial Correlation in Least Squares Regression', *Biometrika*, vol. 38, pp. 159-77.

Engle, R. (1982), 'Autoregressive Conditional Heteroscedasticity with Estimates of the Variance of United Kingdom Inflation', *Econometrica*, vol. 50, pp. 987-1007.

Fama, E. (1981), 'Stock Returns, Real Activity, Inflation and Money', *American Economic Review*, vol. 71, pp. 545-65.

Feige, E.L. (1979), 'How Big is the Irregular Economy?' *Challenge*, November-December, pp. 5-13.

Feige, E.L. (1981), 'The UK's Unobserved Economy: A Preliminary Assessment', *Journal of Economic Affairs*, vol. 1, no. 4, July.

Feige, E.L. (1986), 'A Re-examination of the Underground Economy in the United States: A Comment', *International Monetary Fund Staff Paper*, vol. 33, No. 4, December, pp. 768-81.

Feige, E.L. (1989), *The Underground Economies: Tax Evasion and Information Distortion*, Cambridge, Cambridge University Press.

Feige, E.L. (1996), 'Overseas Holdings of US Currency and the Underground Economy', in Pozo (1996), W.E Upjohn Institute for Employment Research, Michigan, pp. 5-62.

Flexman, B. (1997), 'Canadian Attitudes Towards Taxation' in Lippert, O. and Walker, M. (1997), The Fraser Institute, Vancouver, BC, Canada, pp. 53-74.

Frey, B.S. and Pommerehne, W.W. (1984), 'The Hidden Economy: State and Prospects for Measurement,' *Review of Income and Wealth*, vol. 30, no. 1, pp. 1-23.

Frey, B.S. and Weck-Hannemann, H. (1983), 'Measuring the Hidden Economy: The Case of Switzerland', in Gaertner, W. and Wenig, A. (1985).

Frey, B.S. and Weck-Hannemann, H. (1984), 'The Hidden Economy as An Unobserved Variable', *European Economic Review*, vol. 26, no. 1-2, pp. 33-53.

Frey, B.S., Weck, H. and Pommerehne, W.W. (1982), 'Has the Shadow Economy Grown in Germany? An Exploratory Study,' *Weltwirtschaftliches Archiv*, vol. 118, pp. 499-524.

Friedman, J.H. (1984), 'A Variable Span Smoother', *Technical Report No. 5, Laboratory for Computational Statistics*, Department of Statistics, Stanford University, California.

Gaertner, W. and Wenig, A. (eds) (1985), *The Economics of the Shadow Economy*, Proceeding of the International Conference on the Economics of the Shadow Economy, University of Bielefeld, West Germany, October 10-14, 1983, Springer Verlag, Berlin.

Gaetani-d'Aragona, G. (1981), 'The Hidden Economy: Concealed Labor Markets in Italy', *Rivista-Internazionale-di-Scienze-Economiche-e-Commerciali*, vol. 28, no. 3, pp. 270-80.

Garcia, G. (1978), 'The Currency Ratio and the Subterranean Economy', *Financial Analyst Journal*, November-December, vol. 32, pp. 1-5.

Garcia, G. and Pak, S. (1979), 'The Ratio of Currency to Demand Deposits in the United States', *The Journal of Finance*, June, vol. 34, pp. 703-715.

Gershuny, J.I. (1979), 'The Informal Economy: Its role in the Post-Industrial Society', *Futures*, vol. 11, pp. 3-15.

Giles, D.E.A. (1997a), 'Testing for Asymmetry in the Measured and Underground Business Cycles', *The Economic Record*, vol. 739, no. 222, pp. 225-232.

Giles, D.E.A. (1999), 'The Canadian Underground and Measured Economies: Granger Causality Results', *University of Victoria Discussion Paper*, EWP9907.

Giles, D.E.A. (1999a), 'The Rise and Fall of the New Zealand Underground Economy: Are Business Cycles Symmetric?', *Applied Economics Letters*, vol. 6, pp. 185-189.

Giles, D.E.A. (1999b), 'Modeling the Hidden Economy and the Tax-Gap in New Zealand', *Empirical Economics*, vol. 24. pp. 621-640.

Giles, D.E.A. (1999c), 'Measuring the Hidden Economy: Implications for Econometric Modelling', *Economic Journal*, vol. 109, pp. F370-F380.

Giles, D.E.A. (2000), 'Simulating the Relationship Between the Hidden Economy and the Tax Level and Tax Mix in New Zealand', in Scully, G.W. and Caragata, P.J. (eds) (2000), Kluwer, Boston.

Grabiner (2000), *The Informal Economy, A Report by Lord Grabiner QC* (into the informal economy in the UK), HM Treasury, London.

Greene, W.H. (1993), *Econometric Analysis*, 3rd edition, USA, Prentice-Hall.

Greenfield, H.I. (1993), *Invisible, Outlawed and Untaxed: America's Underground Economy*, Praeger Publishers, London.

Gutmann, P.M. (1977), 'The Subterranean Economy,' *Financial Analyst Journal*, November-December, pp. 26-34.

Halpern, L. and Wyplosz (eds) (1998), *Hungary: Towards a Market Economy*, Cambridge University Press, MA, Cambridge.

Hansson, I. (1982), 'The Underground Economy in a High Tax Country: The Case of Sweden', in Tanzi, V. (1982), pp. 233-43.

Hansson, I. (1989), 'The Underground Economy in Sweden', in Feige, E.L. (1989).

Harding, P. and Jenkins, R. (1989), *The Myth of the Hidden Economy*, Open University Press, Philadelphia.

Hausman, J.A. (1978), 'Specification Tests in Econometrics', *Econometrica*, vol. 46, pp. 1251-72.

Henry, S. (1981), *Can I have it in Cash?: A Study of Informal Institutions and Unorthodox Ways of Doing Things*, Satragal Books, London.

Hill, R. and Kabir, M. (1996), 'Tax Rates, the Tax Mix and the Growth of the Underground Economy in Canada: What Can We Infer?' *Canadian Tax Journal*, vol. 44, no. 6, pp. 1552-83.

Hill, T.P. (1979), 'Do-it-yourself and GDP', *Review of Income and Wealth*, vol. 25, pp. 31-9.

Horowirtz, J.L. (1997), 'Bootstrap Methods in Econometrics: Theory and Numerical Performance', in Kreps, D.M. and Wallis, K.F. (eds) (1997),

Seventh World Congress of the Econometric Society, Keio University, Tokyo (1995), vol. 3.

Houston, J.F. (1987), 'The Underground Economy: A Troubling Issue For Policymakers', *Business Review – Federal Reserve Bank of Philadelphia Working Paper*, vol. 87-9, September-October.

Houston, J.F. (1990), 'The Policy Implications of the Underground Economy', *Journal of Economics & Business*, vol. 42, no. 1, pp. 27-37.

Hunt, J. (1999), 'Has Work-Sharing Worked in Germany?' *Quarterly Journal of Economics*, vol. 89, no. 1, pp. 117-48.

Inland Revenue (IR) (1999), The Challenges to Tax Compliance (Chapter 5), (http://www.inlandrevenue.gov.uk/taxagenda/).

Inland Revenue Department (IRD) (1999), Tax Compliance – Report to the Treasurer and Minister of Revenue by a Committee of Experts on Tax Compliance, IRD, (http://www.taxpolicy.ird.govt.nz/publications/).

Insurance Council of Australia (ICA) (1992), *Bulletin*, May.

Internal Revenue Service (IRS) (1979), *Estimates of Income Unreported on Individual Income Tax Returns*, Washington DC, Government Printing Office.

Isachsen, A.J., Klovland, J.T. and Strom, S. (1982), 'The Hidden Economy in Norway', in Tanzi, V. (1982), Massachusetts, Lexington Books, pp. 209-31.

Isachsen, A.J. and Strom, S. (1985), 'The Size and Growth of the Hidden Economy in Norway', *Review of Income and Wealth*, vol. 3, no. 1, pp. 21-38.

Isachsen, A.J. and Strom, S. (1989), 'The Hidden Economy in Norway With Special Emphasis on the Hidden Labour Market', in Feige, E.L. (ed.) (1989), Cambridge, Cambridge University Press.

Karoleff, V., Mirus, R. and Smith, R.S. (1993), 'Canada's Underground Economy Revisited: Updates and Critique', paper presented at the 49th congress of the International Institute of Public Finance, Berlin, August 1993.

Kaufmann, D., Johnson, S. and Shleifer, A. (1997), 'The Unofficial Economy in Transition', *Brooking Papers in Economic Activity*, vol. 2, pp. 159-221.

Kaufmann, D., Johnson, S. and Zoido-Lobaton, P. (1998), 'Regulatory Discretion and the Unofficial Economy', *American Economic Review*, vol. 88, no. 2, pp. 387-92.

Kaufmann, D. and Kaliberda, A. (1996), 'Integrating the Unofficial Economy into the Dynamics of Post Socialist Economies: A Framework of Analyses and Evidence', *World Bank Policy Research Working Paper*, no. 1691.

Kesselman, J.R. (1997), 'Policy Implications of Tax Evasion and the Underground Economy', in Lippert, O. and Walker, M. (1997), pp. 293-317.

Kinsey, K.A. (1987), 'Survey Data on Tax Compendium and Review', *American Bar Foundation Working Paper*, No. 8716, Chicago.

Kirchgaessner, G. (1981), 'Verfahren zur Erfassung der Grobe und Entwicklung des Schatteensektors, Eidgenossische Technische Hochschule Zurich, November, cited in Frey, B.S., Weck, H. and Pommerehne, W.W. (1982), *Weltwirtschaftliches Archiv*, vol. 118, pp. 499-524.

Kirchgaessner, G. (1983), 'Size and Development of the West German Show

Economy, 1955-1980', *Zeitschrift fur die gesamte Saat-swissenschaft*, vol. 139, pp. 197-214.

Klovland, J.T. (1984), 'Tax Evasion and the Demand for Currency in Norway and Sweden. Is there a Hidden Relationship?', *Scandinavian Journal of Economics*, vol. 86, no. 4, pp. 423-39.

Koopmans, C.C. (1994), 'Direct Measurement of Hidden Labour', *Applied Economics*, vol. 26, pp. 575-81.

Kreps, D.M. and Wallis, K.F. (1997), *Advances in Economics and Econometrics: Theory and Applications*, Seventh World Congress of the Econometric Society, Keio University, Tokyo (1995), vol. 3.

Lacko, M. (1996), 'Hidden Economy in Eastern European Countries in International Comparison', *International Institute for Applied Systems Analysis Working Paper*, Laxenburg.

Lacko, M. (1998), 'The Hidden Economies of Visegrad Countries in International Comparison: A Household Electricity Approach', in Halpern and Wyplosz, (eds) (1998), pp. 128-52.

Lacko, M. (1999), 'Hidden Economy an Unknown Quantity? Comparative Analysis of the Hidden Economies in Transition Countries in 1989-95', *University of Linz Economics Working Paper*, no. 9905, Austria.

Langfelt, E. (1982), 'The Unobserved Economy in the Federal Republic of Germany: A Preliminary Assessment', *Paper Presented for the International Conference on the Unobserved Economy*, Netherlands Institute for Advanced Study, Wassenaar, June.

Langfelt, E. (1989), 'The Underground Economy in the Federal Republic of Germany: A Preliminary Assessment', in Feige. E.L. (1989), Cambridge, Cambridge University Press.

Lemieux, T., Fortin, B. and Frechette, P. (1994), 'The Effects of Taxes on Labour Supply in the Underground Economy', *American Economic Review*, vol. 84. no. 1, pp. 231-54.

Lieberman, C. (1979), 'Structural and Technological Change in Money Demand', *American Economic Review*, vol. 69, no. 2, pp. 324-29.

Lippert, O. and Walker, M. (1997), *The Underground Economy: Global Evidence of Its Size and Impact*, The Fraser Institute, Vancouver, BC, Canada.

Loayza, N.V. (1996), 'The Economics of the Informal Sector: A Simple Model and Some Empirical Evidence for Latin America', *Carnegie-Rochester Conference Series in Public Policy*, vol. 45, pp. 129-62.

Macafee, K. (1980), 'A Glimpse of the Hidden Economy in the National Accounts', *Economic Trends*, February, vol. 316, p. 81.

MacKinnon, J., White, G.H. and Davidson, R. (1983), 'Tests for Model Specification in the Presence of Alternative Hypothesis: Some Further Results', *Journal of Econometrics*, vol. 21, pp. 53-70.

Matthews, K.G.P. (1982), 'The Demand for Currency and the Black Economy in the UK', *Journal of Economic Studies*, vol. 9, no. 2, pp. 3-22.

Matthews, K.G.P. (1984), 'The GDP Residual Error and the Black Economy: A Note', *Applied Economics*, vol. 16, pp. 443-48.

McDonald, R.J. (1984), The Underground Economy and BLS Statistics Data, *Monthly Labour Review*, January, pp. 4-18.

Mirus, R. and Smith, R.S. (1989), 'Canada's Underground Economy', in Feige, E.L. (1989), Cambridge, Cambridge University Press.

Mirus, R., Smith, R.S. and Karoleff, V. (1994), 'Canada's Underground Economy Revisited: Update and Critique', *Canadian Public Policy*, vol. 20, no. 3, pp. 235-52.

Mogensen, G.V., Kvist, H.K., Kormendi, E. and Pedersen, S. (1995), 'The Shadow Economy in Denmark 1994: Measurement and Results', Study no. 3, Rockwool Foundation Research Unit, Copenhagen.

Moreno, R. (1992), 'Macroeconomic Shocks and Business Cycles in Australia', *Economic Review*, vol. 3, pp. 34-52.

Myrsten, K. (1989), 'Det illegala bygghantverket', Brattsutveckligen (L. Johansson, Ed.), *Brattsforebyggande Kadet*, Stockholm, in Hasson, I. (1989).

National Bureau of Economic Research (NBER) (1992), 'Recessions', *National Bureau of Economic Research Public Information Office Release.*

OECD (1978), *Methods Used To Estimate the Extent of Tax Evasion*, Mimeo vol. 78, no. 6, Paris, November 17.

OECD (1980), Une etude sur l'exactitude des declarations de revenus en France, Mimeo, MAS/WP.7, vol. 80, no. 3, March, Paris cited in Frey. B.S. and Pommerehne, W.W. (1984).

O'Higgins, M. (1981), 'Aggregate Measurement of Tax Evasion: An Assessment', *British Tax Review*, vol. 5, pp. 286-302.

O'Higgins, M. (1985), 'The Relationship between the Formal and Hidden Economies: An Exploratory Analysis for Four Countries', in Gaertner, W. and Wenig, A. (1985), Proceeding of the International Conference on the Economics of the Shadow Economy, University of Bielefeld, West Germany, October 10-14, 1983, Springer Verlag, Berlin.

O'Higgins, M. (1989), 'Assessing the Underground Economy in the United Kingdom', in Feige, E.L. (1989), Cambridge, Cambridge University Press.

O'Neill, D.M. (1983), 'Growth of the Underground Economy (1950-81): Some Evidence from the Current Population Survey', Study from the Joint Economic Committee, No. 98:122, US Government Printing Office, Washington DC.

Pagan, A.R. and Volker, P.A. (1981), 'The Short-Run Demand for Transaction Balances in Australia', *Economica*, vol. 48, pp. 381-95.

Park, T. (1979), 'Reconciliation Between Personal Income and Taxable Income (1947-1977)', Mimeo, Bureau of Economic Analysis, Washington DC, May, cited in Frey, B.S. and Pommerehne, W.W. (1984), *Review of Income and Wealth*, vol. 30, no. 1, pp. 1-23.

Pestiau, P. (1983), 'Belgium's Irregular Economy', in Gaertner, W. and Wenig, A. (1985), Proceeding of the International Conference on the Economics of the

Shadow Economy, University of Bielefeld, West Germany, October 10-14, 1983, Springer Verlag, Berlin.

Petersen H.G. (1982), 'Size of the Public Sector, Economic Growth and The Informal Economy: Development Trends in The Federal Republic of Germany,' *Review of Income and Wealth*, vol. 28, pp. 191-215.

Phillips, P.C.B. and Ouliaris, S. (1990), 'Asymptotic Properties of Residual Based Tests for Cointegration', *Econometrica*, vol. 58, pp. 165-193.

Porter, R.D. and Bayer, A.S. (1989), 'Monetary Perspective on Underground Economic Activity in the United States,' in Feige, E.L. (1989).

Portes, A., Castells, M. and Benton, L. (1989), *The Informal Economy: Studies in Advanced and Less Developed Countries*, Johns Hopkins University Press, Baltimore.

Potas, I., Vining, A. and Wilson, P. (1990), *Young People and Crime: Cost and Prevention*, Australian Institute of Criminology, Canberra.

Pozo, S. (1996), *Exploring The Underground Economy: Studies of Illegal and Unreported Activity*, W.E Upjohn Institute for Employment Research, Michigan.

Pozo, S. (1996a), *Price Behaviour in Illegal Markets*, Avebury, Aldershot.

Prager, J. (1983), 'Two Cheers for the Underground Economy', *Economic Policy Papers*, Centre for Applied Economics, New York University.

Priest, G. (1994), 'The Ambiguous Moral Foundations of the Underground Economy', *Yale Law Journal*, vol. 103, no. 8. pp. 2259-88.

Ramsey, J.B. (1969), ' Tests for Specification Errors in Classical Linear Least Squares Regression Analysis', *Journal of Royal Statistical Society*, Series B, vol. 31, pp. 350-371.

Reed, M. (1985), 'An Alternative View of the Underground Economy', *Journal of Economic Issues*, vol. 19, no. 2, pp. 567-73.

Reuter, P. (1982), 'The Irregular Economy and The Quality of Macroeconomic Statistics', in Tanzi, V. (ed) (1982), pp. 125-143.

Revenue Canada (RC) (1999), Revenue Canada: Underground Economy Initiative, *1999 Report of the Auditor General*, April (web-site: http://www. oag-bvg.gc.ca/).

Riebel, V. (1984), 'Arbeitszeitverkurzung und Schwarzarbeit: Auswirkungen einer Verkurzung der Wochenarbeitszeit auf das individuelle Arbeitsangebot, cited in Schneider, F. and Enste, D.H (2000), *Journal of Economic Literature*, vol. 38, pp. 77-114.

Ross, I. (1978), 'Why the Underground Economy is Booming', *Fortune*, October, pp. 92-8.

Schneider, F. (1986), 'Estimating the Size of the Danish Shadow Economy Using The Currency Demand Approach: An Attempt', *Scandinavian Journal of Economics*, vol. 88, no. 4, pp. 643-668.

Schneider, F. (1994a), 'Measuring the Size and Development of the Shadow Economy: Can the Causes be Found and the Obstacles Overcome?', in

Brandstaetter, H. and Guth, W. (1994), Berlin: Springer, Germany, pp. 193-212.

Schneider, F. (1994b), 'Can the Shadow Economy be Reduced Through Major Tax Reforms? An Empirical Investigation for Austria', Supplement to Public Finance, vol. 49, pp. 137-52.

Schneider, F. (1997), 'The Shadow Economies of Western Europe', *Journal of the Institute Economic Affairs*, vol. 17, no. 3, pp. 42-8.

Schneider (1998a), 'Further Empirical Results of the Size of the Shadow Economy of 17 OECD Countries Over Time', Paper presented at the 54th Congress of IIPF, Cordoba, Argentina.

Schneider, F. (1999), 'The Interaction of Taxes, Transfers and Growing Shadow Economies – What are the Causes?: An Empirical (Public Choice Orientated) Analysis', *ATAX Discussion Paper*, Faculty of Law, UNSW.

Schneider, F. and Enste, D.H. (2000), 'Shadow Economies: Size, Causes and Consequences', *Journal of Economic Literature*, vol. 38, pp. 77-114.

Schramn, I. (1990), Police paper presented to the 1990 National Conference of the Australian Institute of Credit Management, Adelaide, as reported by the Advertiser, September.

Schwartz, G. (1978), 'Estimating the Dimensions of a Model', *The Annuals of Statistics*, vol. 6, pp. 461-64.

Scully, G.W. and Caragata, P.J. (eds) (2000), *Taxation and The Limits of Government*, Kluwer, Boston.

Seeman, R. (1984), 'Tax Cheats', *The Japan Lawletter*, April.

Silvapulle, P. and Silvapulle, M.J. (1997), 'Business Cycle Asymmetry and The Stock Market', *La Trobe University Discussion Paper*, No. A.97.22.

Simon, C.P. and Witte, A.D. (1982), *Beating the System: The Underground Economy*, Auburn House, Boston, USA.

Skolka, J. (1984), 'A Few Facts About the Hidden Economy Seminar – The Unofficial Economy, Consequences and Policies in the West and East', cited in Mirus, R. Smith, R.S. and Karoleff, V. (1984), *Canadian Public Policy*, vol. 20, no. 3, pp. 235-52.

Smith, P.M. (1997), 'Assessing The Size of The Underground Economy: The Statistics Canada Perspective', in Lippert, O. and Walker, M. (1997).

Smith, S., Pissarides, C.A. and Weber, G. (1986), 'Evidence for Survey Discrepancies', in Smith S. and Weid-Nebbeling, S. (1986).

Smith, S. and Weid-Nebbeling, S. (1986), *The Shadow Economy in Britain and Germany*, Anglo-German Foundation, London.

Spiro, P.S. (1993), 'Evidence of a Post-GST Increase in the Underground Economy', *Canadian Tax Journal*, vol. 41, no. 2, pp. 247-58.

Stock, J.H. and Watson, M.W. (1998), 'Business Cycle Fluctuations in Macroeconomic Time Series', *NBER Working Paper Series*, No. 6528.

Tanzi, V. (1980), 'The Underground Economy in the United States: Estimates and Implications', *Banca Nazionale del Lavoro (Rome)*, vol. 135, December, pp. 427-53.

Tanzi, V. (1982), *The Underground Economy in the United States and Abroad*, Massachusetts, Lexington Books.

Tanzi, V. (1983), 'The Underground Economy in the United States: Annual Estimates, 1930-1980', *International Monetary Fund Staff Papers*, vol. 30, pp. 283-305.

Taylor, N. (2000), 'Why Should I Pay Tax? Understanding the Motivations of Taxpayers Through Looking at What They Say', Paper presented at CTSI's 1st International Conference on Building a Cooperative Taxpaying Culture, Australian National University, Canberra, December 4-5.

Terasvirta, T. (1990), 'Generalizing Threshold Autoregressive Models', *University of California Discussion Paper*, No. 90-44.

Thomas, J.J. (1992), *Informal Economic Activity*, London School of Economics Handbook in Economics, Harvester Wheatsheaf, London.

Thurman, Q.C., St John, C. and Riggs, L. (1984), 'Neutralisation and Tax Evasion: How Effective Would a Moral Appeal Be In Improving Compliance to Tax Laws?' *Law and Policy*, vol. 6, no. 3, pp. 309-27.

Tong, H. (1990), *Non-Linear Time Series: A Dynamic System Approach*, Oxford University Press, Oxford.

Ullah, A. and Giles, D. (eds) (1998), *Handbook of Applied Economic Statistics*, Marcel Kekker, New York.

Van Eck, R. and Kazemier, B. (1988), 'Features of the Hidden Economy in Netherlands', *Review of Income and Wealth*, vol. 34, pp. 251-73.

Van Wel, C. (1998), 'Recent Australian Business Cycles', *Economic Papers*, vol. 17, no. 2, pp. 1-12.

Veall, M.R. (1998), 'Application of the Bootstrap in Econometrics and Economic Statistics', in Ullah, A. and Giles, D. (eds) (1998).

Watson, M.W. (1994), 'Business Cycle Durations and Postwar Stabilisation of the US Economy', *The American Economic Review*, vol. 84, no. 1, pp. 24-46.

Williams, C.C. and Windebank, J. (1995), 'Black Market Work in the European Community: Peripheral Work for Peripheral Localities?', *International Journal of Urban and Regional Research*, vol. 19, no. 1, pp. 23-9.

Yoo, T. and Hyun, J.K. (1998), 'International Comparison of the Black Economy: Empirical Using Micro-Level Data', Paper presented at the 1998 Congress of International Institute of Public Finance, Cordoba, Argentina.

Zilberfarb, B.Z. (1986), 'Estimates of the Underground Economy in the United States: A Comment on Tanzi', *International Monetary Fund Staff Papers*, vol. 33, no. 4, December, pp. 790-98.

Index

Audit 4, 14, 26, 30-31, 49, 57, 81, 107-108, 128, 141, 147-150, 152, 154, 161
Australian Bureau Statistics (ABS) 2-3, 15, 17-18, 32, 77, 168
Australian Business Number (ABN) 11, 42, 72, 107-110, 117, 121, 169
Australian National Accounts (ANA) 2-3, 15, 19, 20
Australian Taxation Office (ATO) 2, 4, 8-10, 22, 30, 48, 58, 71, 107-110, 126, 128-130, 154-165, 171
Average tax rates 59, 68, 79, 115, 122

Bajada, C. 17
Barthelemy, P. 35, 39
Baumol, W.J. 35
Baxter, M. 90
Belgium 29
Bhattacharyya, D.K. 6, 24, 35, 40
Blades, D. 19
Boehm, E.A. 90
Bootstrap 82-85
Boschan, C. 90
Bracket creep 46
Britain 11, 29
Building 30, 153, 157-158
Burns, A.F. 90-91
Business Activity Statement (BAS) 107
Business cycle 3, 9-10, 12, 14-15, 45, 52, 71, 74, 76, 78-79, 90-92, 94-96, 98-100, 119, 166-169
Business expenditures 26
Business-to-business transactions 107, 109
Business-to-consumer transactions 108-110

Cafes 30, 129, 157
Cagan, P. 34
Canada 5, 7, 11, 33, 35, 37-39, 43, 51, 74, 107, 138, 148-153, 169, 171
Canadian Customs and Revenue Agency 151
Carson, C.S. 19, 48, 52, 55
Carter, M. 33, 51, 55, 57, 79
Cash Economy Task Force (CETF) 9, 25, 71, 154-155, 157, 160, 162, 164-165, 171
Catering 20
Classical cycle 92
Cleaning 23, 127
Clothing 4, 10, 30, 141, 157-158, 164
Company tax 146
Competition 9, 47, 52, 55, 167, 169
Compliance initiatives 26, 147
Compliance model 156, 160-161
Confidence interval 62, 69, 82-85, 88-89
Consequences 11, 14-15, 18, 41, 50, 57, 125, 143, 147, 155, 160, 162-163, 166-167
Construction 30, 126, 129-130, 150, 152, 157-158, 170
Consumer-to-consumer transactions 108, 110
Consumption 14, 18, 21, 23, 36, 53, 58-62, 69-70, 73-75, 112, 116
Contini, B. 32
Contractionary phase 90, 92
Coyotes 5
Credit card 12, 14, 22, 58
Creditable purchases 107
Crime 22, 58
Criminal activities 6, 8, 19, 22-23, 27, 58, 142
Currency 13-14, 33-35, 57-69, 71, 73, 82-83, 85, 111-116, 166-167
Currency demand 34-35, 59-60, 62-63, 65-66, 68, 82-83, 111-112, 114, 167
Currency substitutes 166

Cycles 45, 70-71, 74-75, 78-79, 90-91, 95, 100, 168

Data protection laws 142
Davidson, R. 63, 112
Debit cards 12, 14
Decorating 20, 23, 126, 141
Demand deposits 34, 59, 73
Denmark 30, 44
Department of Social Security 142
Dilnot, A. 106, 120, 146
Disposable income 6, 10, 15, 22, 26, 41, 44-49, 54, 59-62, 64, 67, 79, 111-114, 121-122, 124, 139
Do-it-yourself 8, 166
Drug trafficking 6, 8, 19, 24

E-commerce 140
Economic cycle 9, 71, 100
Economic development 55
Economic fluctuations 46
Economic growth 10, 52, 55, 64, 72, 119, 146
EFTPOS 14
Elasticity 36, 125, 127-130
Electrician 21
Electricity consumption 36
Electronic payments 12, 14
Electronic substitutes 58
Employment 20, 30, 45, 47-48, 53-54, 91, 140, 147, 159, 168
Enforcement 23, 42, 52, 142, 146, 150, 161, 165, 167
Error Correction Mechanism (ECM) 62, 112
Expansionary phase 90, 92
Expenditure 3, 18, 21, 31-32, 41, 53, 58-62, 73, 75, 109, 112, 119-120, 168
Expenses 1, 4-5, 8, 18, 21, 31

Federal budget 107
Feige, E.L. 6, 22-24, 33-35, 39, 79, 139
Financial ratios 107-108, 159
Financial sector 59
First Homebuyer Scheme 73
Fiscal auditing 31
Fiscal policy 121, 170
Flexman, B. 43

Fluctuations 3, 12, 62, 69, 71, 74, 76, 81, 95, 167
Forecasting 9
France 30
Fraud 6, 21-22, 115, 140-144, 147
Fraudulent claims 140
Frey B.S. 6, 24, 30, 32-33, 35, 37, 46, 48-50, 55, 74, 81, 139,
Friedman, J.H. 94

Gambling 18-19
Garcia, G. 34, 73, 79
Gardening 4, 23
Germany 6, 30-31, 37-40, 44, 49, 74, 81
Giles, D.E.A. 26, 35, 51, 55, 74, 90, 94, 107, 146
Goods and services 2, 3, 10-12, 18-19, 41, 52-53, 55, 59, 64, 107, 110, 115, 123, 167, 171
Goods and Services Tax (GST) 11, 42-43, 53, 61-62, 70, 72-73, 106-107, 109-112, 118-119, 121-124, 129, 138-139, 146, 148-151, 153, 164, 167-170
Grabiner 140-142, 144
Greenfield, H.I. 50, 52, 55
Gross Domestic Product (GDP) 2-3, 7, 12, 15, 17-19, 27, 36, 38-39, 59-61, 68-71, 73-74, 76-79, 86-88, 92, 94-96, 98-99, 115-119, 122-124, 128-129, 146, 168-170
Gross tax gap 23
Growth cycle 94
Gutmann, P. 11, 24, 33-34, 39, 57, 73-74

Hairdressing 20, 127-128
Hansson, I. 6, 29, 31, 38, 52-53
Harding, P. 55
Harmonized Sales Tax (HST) 148
Holland 30
Home-based production 158
Horowitz, J.L. 82
Household repairs 8
Household sector 2, 36, 106, 116-118, 169
Household transactions 108, 110-111, 115, 117-119

Index

Housework 23
Housing construction 126, 138, 162, 170
Houston, J.F 49, 52, 120, 122
Human capital 53

Illegal currency 69, 85, 116
Immigrants 5, 141, 147
Immigration 5
Income effect 75
Income inequality 54
Income tax 2, 4, 20, 23, 34, 44, 48, 61, 112, 115, 125-126, 128, 140, 144-145, 148-149, 151, 160, 165
Income tax returns 2, 145, 148, 160, 165
Indirect taxes 43, 124, 146, 170
Inflation 2, 13, 33, 42, 46, 52, 55, 59, 60-61, 79, 113, 146, 161
Informal Economy Report 143
Inland Revenue Department 147
Input tax credit 107, 109, 110
Insurance fraud 22
Internet 140
Interviews 29, 159
Invoice splitting 109
Isachsen, A.J. 30
Italy 29, 32, 37-40

Japan 5

Kauffman, D. 36
Kesselman, J.R. 53, 55
King, R. 90
Kinsey, K.A. 30, 81
Kirchgaessner, G. 44
Klovland, J.T. 30, 44

Labour market 32, 43-45, 81
Lacko, M. 36
Langfelt, E. 31-32, 38, 81
Laundering 19, 27, 154
Legal currency 68
Legitimate businesses 47, 52, 148
Loan sharking 19

Macafee, K. 24, 31-32, 35, 37, 139
Manufacturing 22, 126, 129
Matthews, K.P.G. 31, 33
McDonald, R.J. 52

Medicare 107
Mirus, R. 6, 24, 31-33, 38
Mitchell, W. 90, 91
Money supply 58
Moonlighting 42
Morris, C.N. 29, 35, 38, 74, 81
Myrsten, K. 32, 38, 81

National accounts 1, 3, 6, 8, 18-20, 22-24, 26-27, 31-32, 51, 71, 118-119, 168
National Bureau of Economic Research (NBER) 91
National Crime Authority 58
New Zealand 11, 35, 51, 74, 90, 94, 107, 138, 146-148, 169, 171
Norway 29, 35, 44

Opportunity cost 59, 64, 113
Overtime 49
Owner occupied dwellings 23

Pagan, A.R. 58
Painting 20, 23, 127
Pareto Improvement 3, 110
Pay-As-You-Earn (PAYE) 139
Pay-As-You-Go (PAYG) 107
Payroll tax 20, 150
Pestiau, P. 29, 81
Petersen, H.G. 6, 38, 74
Pommerehne, W.W. 6, 24, 30, 32, 34-35, 37, 48, 50, 74, 81
Portes, A. 55
Pozo, S. 23, 55
Prager, J. 55
Prescribed Payments System (PPS) 158
Primary production 10, 125, 129-130
Private dwellings 18
Productivity 22, 52, 53
Progressive income tax 42, 44
Provincial Sales tax (PST) 148
Public officials 57
Public perception 60, 118, 119, 146, 170

Ratchet effect 43
Recession 9, 12, 73
Regulation 10, 35, 44, 49, 125, 146, 159-160, 171

Rent 21, 23
Reportable Payments System (RPS) 130, 158
RESET 35, 65, 113-114
Resident businesses 112, 115-116
Restaurants 30, 129, 157
Retail trade 129-130
Reuter, P. 52, 138
Revenue Canada 149-153
Reverse searches 143
Risk preference 45
Road transport 30

Sales tax evasion 159
Schneider, F. 25-26, 34, 36-40, 44, 55
Self-employed 21, 143
Services 3, 6, 8, 12, 19-22, 30-31, 33, 52-53, 55, 59, 68, 74, 107, 109-110, 126-129, 156, 162, 165, 168, 170
Simon, C.P. 30, 81
Skolka, J. 54, 55
Smith, S. 6, 19, 24, 31-33, 38, 107
Smuggling 5, 19
Social security 34, 47, 142, 155, 169
Sole traders 126
Spiro, P.S. 107
Statistical discrepancy 32
Statistics Canada 7
Strom, S. 30
Sub-contracting 47
Substitution effect 33, 74, 79, 168
Surveys 29-31, 44, 58, 81, 149, 154
Sweden 6, 30-31, 35, 37-38, 44, 74, 81

Tanzi, V. 6, 24, 33-34, 39, 55, 74, 79
Tax avoidance 1, 48, 110, 170
Tax burden 3, 6, 44, 59-60, 120-127, 161, 167
Tax collections 1, 11, 73, 124, 139
Tax evasion 1-2, 5-6, 14-15, 19, 23, 26, 41, 45-46, 48, 51, 53, 57, 109, 129, 139-140, 142, 145, 147-150, 152, 154, 158-162, 164-165, 169

Tax incidence 106, 120, 124
Tax mix 70, 73, 139, 146
Tax moral index 35
Tax practitioners 148, 155
Tax reform 11, 42, 72, 106-108, 111, 119, 122, 169-171
Tax revenue 2-3, 6, 9, 11, 19, 21, 23-24, 27, 51, 60, 110, 120, 124-125, 150, 167-169
Tax-free threshold 42
Taxi 10, 30, 127, 129, 160, 170
Terasvirta, T. 94
Theft 8, 22
Thomas, J.J. 31, 55
Threshold models 93, 100
Tobin, J. 35
Transfer payments 9

Unemployment benefits 21, 45, 46, 47, 76, 77
United Kingdom 6, 30-31, 35, 107, 138, 139, 169, 171
United Nations 17, 18
United States 5-6, 12, 29, 30-35, 57, 81, 89, 142
Unrecorded activities 23, 169
Unreported income 79, 107

Value Added Tax 107, 139, 141
Veall, M.R. 82
Velocity 69, 116
Volker, P.A. 58
Voluntary compliance 48, 150, 156-157, 163

Wage and salary earners 112, 115-116, 120, 126-127
Waitress 20
Watson, M.W. 65, 90-91, 114
Welfare assistance 54, 142
Welfare benefit fraud 23, 162
White, G.H. 63, 112
Witte, A.D. 30, 37, 81